I Play With Giants

Mike Roche

PUNK ★ HOSTAGE ★ PRESS

I Play With Giants

Copyright © 2024 Mike Roche
Published by Punk Hostage Press
ISBN: 978-1-940213-27-9

All rights reserved. Printed in the United States of America. No part of this text may be used or reproduced in any manner whatsoever without written permission from the author or publisher except in the case of brief quotations embodied in critical articles and reviews. For information, address: Punk Hostage Press,
Los Angeles, California.

Foreword
Jack Grisham

Editors
Melissa Elhardt
Tracy Vaughan
Richard Modiano

Photo Credits
Cover photo – Roche Family Archives
Back cover photo – Tony Smith Images

Cover Art & Layout
Julia Kwong

Punk ★ Hostage ★ Press
Los Angeles, California
www.punkhostagepress.com

The Story I've told in the pages and chapters of this book are true. These moments were some of the highest, and lowest points during a certain period of my life.

Mike Roche, 2024

CONTENTS

FOREWORD	ix
EARLY YEARS	1
INFINITY	7
EARLY PUNK ROCK IN HB & LB	11
THE BEGINNING OF TSOL	15
GOLDENVOICE	23
EARLY SHOWS & TOURING	27
SOMEWHERE IN MIDDLE AMERICA	35
MEETING MY MENTOR	39
SUBURBIA	43
THE BEGINNING OF THE END	47
ELECTRIC CHAIR	49
CHANGE TODAY	53
THE REUNION	63
HIGH DESERT	73
LA RIOTS	81
ELVIS	85
PRISON BOUND	89
SOBRIETY	95
SOCIAL CHAOS & TATTOOING	101
BACK TO PUNK ROCK	107
HART & HUNTINGTON	113
A NEW DECADE	117
LOVE AND LOSS	123
UNDER THE INFLUENCE	127
TWENTY TWENTY	129
AGAINST ALL ODDS	133
IN CLOSING GIANTS	135
MORE ABOUT THE BOOK	137
HONORABLE MENTIONS	139
ACKNOWLEDGMENTS	141
MORE ABOUT THE AUTHOR	142
MORE BOOKS ON PUNK HOSTAGE PRESS	144

FOREWORD

The Man with the Plan

You can never be too smart for your own good. Lesser men created that phrase—cretins attempting to disguise their lack of balls by spitting out cautionary tales of soulless self-destruction. They could only wish that they had the wit and the fortitude to take on the world. And so what if you pull it all down around you—if your friends hate you and the police paint a target on your back big enough for their beady little eyes to hone in on. Good. Bring it. Let 'em come. I mean, look, kids. Mike broke his fucking dog out of jail. That alone gives him hero status. It's the final salvo in any argument—"Oh yeah, well, did you ever break your dog out of jail?" Bye-bye, walk away. Chuck Norris himself can't claim that. "Yeah, you might've kicked Bruce Lee's ass, but you never…"

I met Mike sometime around 1979. The punk rock experience was beginning to bloom in Orange County and vicious genius was on the vine. Mike was a surfer—supposedly pretty good, but I never witnessed it. I did however take note of the shaggy cropped hairdo, the snaggle teeth, and the impeccable style—peg leg pants, Beatle boots, leather jacket, and a wicked tan. Mike was a ladies man—(can you say that these days? No? Well, fuck you. You weren't there so you didn't see the chain of salivating sweethearts that swung behind him.) Mike was somebody in a world of misfits. He was that dangerous intelligent boy that the straight teen sluts wanted to get close to—you know, frighten mommy and daddy with bad romantic choices. Mike was also the man with a plan and that's where I come in.

I was sucked into one of his schemes. He needed a singer for a pop group that he played bass for and I fit the bill. It was a quasi-political outfit with anarchist leanings. Now, getting back to that too-smart business. If, we as individuals, acted in a vacuum; meaning if the populace of the world was bright enough to acknowledge our higher understanding of life and the universe, and they blindly did whatever we said, our great intelligence could be utilized for the benefit of all.

However, that's not the case. These lumps of human flesh become roadblocks to our greatness. They stumble over our playbook, and they clog the arteries of invention with their small-minded refusal to act as we need them to act…oh yeah, and drugs. Did I mention drugs—alcohol, meth, heroin, uppers, downers, and any other mood, or mind-altering, substance that one ingests to deal with the frustration of having subjects that don't follow the orders of the Most High?

Yeah, Mike might've played with giants, walked among them, and lurched over them, but he was the one with the plan, and while it might not have served him as he wished, his rise, fall, and humbling resurrection from the pit does make for an extremely fun—albeit gut-wrenching read.

— Jack Grisham

*I've been a creator, entrepreneur, artist, surfer,
musician, and friend.
A junkie, thief, liar, robber, burglar,
convict and back again.
Mike Roche*

It was a cold rainy night in December of 2018, and we'd just finished playing a sold-out show at the Observatory. It's a great room and my favorite venue in Orange County. My career would be much different today; in fact, my life would be much different if every room we played was the Observatory. The show was great! There was the perfect amount of chaos; with Jack as the ultimate ringmaster running the show, always playing the crowd as much as we all played the songs.

After one of the best shows in my career, I was standing out back, trying to smoke a cigar in the rain, visiting with old and new friends, signing an occasional hat or record, and taking pictures. I was really enjoying the night, my life, and what it had become. As I stood there, a tall thin girl walked up with her friend; I knew her. She was visibly crying so I asked, "What's the matter?"

She said, "Hi, I just wanted to apologize to you."

I asked, "Why?"

She said, "Because I have hated you for twenty years."

I questioned, "Hated me? I'm sorry, what did I do, what did I do to you?"

I was puzzled trying to remember if I had hurt her in some way or how.

She said, "You killed my best friend."

EARLY YEARS

I was sleeping on the couch in our house on Kikui Drive, in Huntington Beach when I awoke to my parents talking in a serious manner. Face down on the couch, I opened my eyes and heard my father tell my mom he wanted a divorce. He said, "You undermine my authority with Mike." I felt myself tear up and kept my face buried down in the cushion. I felt horrible hearing him say that it was my fault. The burden of responsibility for a teen to hear this was quite heavy. Little did I know at the time, it was just the beginning and not the end. It was the turning point where everything really began for me, my freedom, my life, as I knew it, and what it has turned out to be.

I don't remember all the details, but I know it was devastating for my mother, and I imagine for my sister, Coleen, as well. The divorce of my parents would turn out to be the most liberating thing that ever happened to me. Up until that point in my life, I was a pretty average kid; surfing, skateboarding, and going to school. We scrambled to keep it together, Coleen, my mom, and myself. We rented a little ghetto apartment in Huntington Beach on the corner of Jaclyn and Liberty Streets. Yes, there are areas in H.B. that aren't that nice. But I was finally free! I loved my newfound freedom; I was finally able to do what I wanted without being under my father's thumb.

I never responded well to my father's authority, nor did we ever connect in a warm fuzzy "Father Knows Best" kind of way. I don't believe my father got who I was, at all. I always felt that I was an older soul than my father. Things that mystified him, in my eyes, seemed simple. In his daily interactions and dealing with people, he seemed to quickly draw a line in the sand. He struggled to achieve and find a balance of what he wanted in life. Maybe it was the responsibility of family and paying the bills, but his focus was always on work, building or racing motorcycles, and preparing for race day at the track. Although according to my mom, there was a pattern of infidelity over the years. That could have been a contributing factor to why my mom and dad were at odds sometimes. I felt like it was a lot about my dad and not so much about us. There was no time spent tossing a ball around or a father-son fishing trip.

I realize now, as an adult, how the responsibilities of husband and father can be overwhelming, and if you're not all in, then there are casualties. I know he did the best he could. We were always taken care of and had a roof over our heads. People have different ways of showing love. His way was taking me to the racetrack with him on Sundays. So, I engaged with him by enjoying watching him on race day. He happened to be very fast and rather good. My father was an AMA expert and held a top 100 number. He was on Green Team Kawasaki and Team BMW. He held track records and dominated locally. However, major success always seemed to be out of his reach. I would hang out in the garage with him and help when and where I could. He was a master at anything mechanical and he even built me a street bike when I was a little older. I, however, wasn't a master of mechanics and as the years went on, I wasn't as interested as he may have wanted me to be.

My grandfather became very sick when my father was young. As his health declined, my dad started acting out. I don't think his parents were able to handle him, so they lied about my father's age to get him into the Navy. I believe his youth was cut short due to this decision. Maybe he never came to terms with the passing of his father so young. There was seemingly a weight, a heaviness that he carried with him; anger underneath it all. His actions toward me were more demoralizing than violent, I thought that was normal and didn't find out for years that it wasn't. He liked to test me, and I hated that. Maybe it was just that I wasn't what he wanted me to be. I was possibly a disappointment or maybe I was more like my mother, and he hated that. Later, I believe he tried to connect with me more, but that ship had sailed. All I wanted to do was surf.

I was born in Santa Maria California in 1961. I have one younger sister, Coleen. We lived in Sacramento, Downey, and even Hawaii for a short time when I was young, as my father searched for his place in the world. My mom had kind of a rough upbringing. She and her brothers were passed along to different in-laws, aunts, uncles, grandparents, etc., as her mother didn't have the ability or interest in raising three children. Despite this adversity, my mom remained kind, loving, generous, and I believe, a great mother. She went on to become a nurse and always fought for me and my sister. She worked, cooked, cleaned, and ran the household, but mostly she worked.

During the early to mid-seventies, my family moved from Downey to Huntington Beach. We lived in an apartment at the end of Ellis Ave., which is behind the Five Points shopping center. A few years later, my parents bought a house less than a mile away from the California coast. We lived on Greenboro Lane, behind the Edison Power plant. It was a great place to grow up. We didn't have much money, but we never went without. The best part about living there was learning how to surf. My first surfboard was a three-dollar piece of junk that I bought at a garage sale. It was horrible and cut me every time I attempted to ride. But it was mine and it was a start.

I didn't really like going to school much, except for art class. My head was always in the clouds. I think I was fairly average for a kid growing up in So Cal; skateboarding, riding my bike, and surfing. I also happened to discover weed at some point, around this time. My folks weren't really drinkers, except for the occasional bottle of vodka in a cupboard for Holidays, etc. I would walk home from school for lunch and take a shot, from time to time, for no particular reason. I would then water the bottle down, so no one would notice any of the contents missing. Then, if I had any weed, I would smoke a little of that too. Hmmm…Smoking and drinking alone?

Had my father known what I was up to, it would have been punishable by death or close to; probably restriction for a month, which meant no surfing. Nonetheless, I continued to do this whenever possible, and believed it was normal to do so in Huntington Beach, or so I thought. I also remember leaving my surfboard at a friend's house because my dad didn't want me surfing before school; he thought it was affecting my grades. So, I would leave early, surf, change at my friend's house and go to school from there. In hindsight, I wasn't very comfortable with myself and was searching, pretty early on, for a way to feel better, or different, even normal or whatever that was. Edison High School in South HB and around that area was where I was first introduced to punk.

As home prices started to soar, my father decided to cash in our house, moving us into a three-bedroom home off Brookhurst, on Kikui Drive and to start a business. Although quite a bit further from the beach, it was still in HB, and I was able to attend Huntington Beach High School. I loved that the school was closer to the beach and downtown, as I had already been hanging around downtown for a while, so it felt much more comfortable to me than Edison. I landed on the varsity surf team and received a letter. I was very proud to have made the team. But, sadly the letter, at the time, meant little or nothing to me. I associated that with the jocks wearing their Letterman jackets. Going to HB high school, the surf team was the best thing going and I don't remember anyone on the varsity surf team wearing a jacket. We were surfers, not jocks. Now, I wish I had kept it, as some kind of token of fond memories. After all, we were the top school on the coast with Coach Hill and Bud Llamas as our fearless leaders. The area seemed to be a more humble, low-key existence with smaller homes, single-parent families, and a working-class kind of vibe, most of which is gone today. I loved downtown; the houses, the neighborhoods, and the locals back when it was a sleepy little surf town. I kept my board at Infinity Surf Shop on PCH and did whatever task was asked of me as a semi part-time job. I made lifelong friends in downtown Huntington, worked hard, played hard, started and lost businesses.

Following my parents' divorce, while living in our two-bedroom apartment on Liberty, my mother continued working at Pacifica Hospital on Delaware St. in HB. I continued to attend Huntington Beach High School. My mom was navigating the dating world, which was brand new to her after so many years of being married. She most certainly was not enjoying these times; her life had been shattered. I, on the other hand, was enjoying my new freedom. I believed we were doing ok. At some point, she met Glen, who swept her off her feet, married her, and moved her to

Tennessee. Glen turned out to be the worst kind of alcoholic. He would be dry for months, if not years, then back to being a violent, black-out drunk. She discovered this long after they were married and living in Tennessee. She later divorced him.

I ended up moving out with my moped and a suitcase to a friend's house. Bob Dixon was a friend of mine, a surfing buddy, and a fellow employee and team rider at Infinity. He came from a big family and was the youngest of several siblings. He was older than me, in his twenties, and we were best of friends. Bob's parents were more like grandparents to me. They were very tolerant, loving, and kind, and gave me much more than I could ever repay. I regret not staying in touch with them and will be forever grateful for all they did for me. By this time, I was going to Wintersburg Continuation School at night and working during the day at Newport Dunes. I would ride my moped every day from Huntington Beach to Newport, and then back in the early evening to make it to school. I was too young to qualify for an apartment. Every time I applied, they looked at me like I was crazy. The Dixons couldn't have been nicer; allowing me to stay with them during these times.

I needed to become an emancipated minor but didn't have the resources or know how to do so. One day on my way home from work, I was pulled over on my moped by HBPD. Supposedly for a fix-it ticket for a broken taillight, that I hadn't taken care of yet. The taillight had, in fact, been fixed, but the ticket still needed to be signed off. So, rather than sign it off or warn me to get it done, to my surprise, this officer decided to arrest me for the fix-it ticket! For the first time ever, I went to the city jail on Main St. in HB, then onto County lock-up (still a juvenile.) I had no relatives nearby or guardian and no way to get out. Luckily Mrs. Emory (mother to Ron, my lifelong best friend) was able to reach my uncle who is an FBI agent. He showed up, pulled some strings and I was released the next day, but not before a stern talking to by the presiding Judge in Chambers. I mean, it was a "fix-it ticket" after all. This would be the beginning of a long and seldom fun history between myself and law enforcement.

I met the Emory brothers while surfing and hanging out in downtown Huntington Beach. Sometimes I would be fishing when they were surfing. Mrs. Emory, Sharon, managed an apartment building at 14th and Olive in HB. When I was seventeen, her oldest son, Bob, and myself rented a two-bedroom apartment next door to hers. Ron (Emory) moved in shortly after. It didn't take long for the three of us to turn the garage from a surfboard shaping and glassing room into a rehearsal room. We started playing guitars and bass whenever we could. We didn't have a clue what we were doing, so we let friends who were in bands rehearse in our garage so we could watch and learn. Mike Ruben an air brusher from a local surf shop, Infinity Surfboards in Huntington, now a NYC-based fashion designer, Doug the drummer, and Chuck the bass player rehearsed pretty much every night in our garage. We were right there watching and trying to soak it all in between beers. Chuck, for whatever reason, left the band and I was in; we were called The Accidents. We played two shows at the Cuckoo's Nest, which should be called the World-Famous Cuckoo's Nest, owned by punk rock champion Jerry Roach (1976-1981) in late '79 or '80, I have no record of the exact dates. Without this place, dozens of bands would've never made it out of their garages, in my opinion. Cuckoo's Nest was the West Coast CBGB's. Countless local bands known today were given an opportunity to play that stage along with some already established acts; Social Distortion, Bad Religion, X, FEAR, 45 Grave, Middle Class, Chiefs, Eddie & The Subtitles, Weirdo's, Circle Jerks, Adolescents, Vandals, China White, JFA, Black Flag, Agent Orange, TSOL, etc., including internationally known acts; Ramones, XTC, Dammed, 999, New York Dolls, Iggy pop, Dead Kennedy's and so on.

INFINITY

I was working full-time as a salesman at Infinity Surfboards after starting as just a kid helping out and hanging around. I loved working at the shop no matter the task at hand. It must've been a year or two later when my manager Dwight Dunn took a job at a new shop around the corner. I was basically left to run things alone, apart from another guy, Jerry Mailing; we were keeping things up and running. The owners, Steve and Barrie Boenhe, a husband-and-wife team, were having a hard time finding a new manager, with some convincing on my part, they let me have the position, and for that, I am forever grateful.

I was almost eighteen and pretty happy to be the youngest manager in the company. Now I have a great job at the beach in a surf town and working in the industry I love. Another local surf shop manager was Bob Hurley, we would have breakfast together often, and times were good. Working at Infinity allowed me to keep the apartment I now shared with Bob and Ron Emory on 14th and Olive, just two blocks from the beach. This may be hard to imagine today, but it was the late seventies, and punk rock wasn't very cool with most folks. However, the older locals and even our high school surf coach were all pretty tolerant with our punk rock leanings.

This particular day at Infinity had begun like any other; a few customers, a few friends, and two of my punk rock surfer buddies were in the shop, getting ready to hit the water. I had let them change in the back where they had left their clothes and keys while they got ready to surf. As they were changing, a man who must've seen them enter the store approached me to ask if he could interview them. I was immediately suspicious, and I asked, "Interview them for who?" He made up some bullshit name and reason and said he knew they were punks, which further confirmed my suspicion. I said, "It's up to them if they want to talk to you, but they have nothing to do with the shop, so it can't happen here." As we spoke further, he persuaded me to let him interview them in the back storeroom. I thought that was fair enough, so I asked Jesse (singer in The Klan) and Doug (drummer in The Accidents) if they were interested in talking to this guy, and they said, "Ya, no problem."

While they were being interviewed in the back storeroom, a theme started to unfold with the type of questions being asked. It appeared the interviewer was interested in punk violence, fights breaking out at shows, carving swastikas in the arms of babies, and other accusations recently reported in the news. These news stories claimed that small children were being held down by gangs of punks and had swastikas carved into their arms. To explain how this insane topic may have come about; in Huntington Beach, at the time, there was a weird fashion or trend to scratch something into your own forearm, barely scratching the surface, lasting a week or two. There were also a select few who fancied the same scar Sid Viscous had on his forearm, which was deeper and much more harsh. Self-inflicted, rare for that time, and pretty stupid. Punk was all about shock value.

So, one interview question went like this: "What about violence at shows?" Jesse responded with, "Anywhere there's booze and lots of drunk people, somebody is bound to get their head kicked in." So, there you have it; he just got his headline. That's all the interviewer wanted; he followed a couple of punks into my surf shop and got the quote he wanted for his interview. He agreed to not use the name, image, or location of the shop in his article. Just as they were leaving, I caught the cameraman filming the front of the shop and signage, so I ran outside and yelled at him. He said he wouldn't use it, and they drove away.

I got a call first thing in the morning from the shop owner. It seemed one of his older surfer friends had caught the headline on the morning news. I remember this like it was yesterday. The expose showed Infinity, my shop, the shop I loved, in a negative light, linked to punk rock violence. Needless to say, my run as the youngest manager was over, thanks to Channel 7 News. I would like to thank Steve and Barrie for trying to keep me on as a shaper during those days. The factory was in Santa Ana, and it just wasn't my thing, so I moved on.

This was my first lesson in how dishonest the media was and is and how punk rock would be treated in the days and years to come. The police seemed to be using large punk shows as a way to practice heavy-handed techniques for crowd control. The crowd being a large group of kids at shows. The cops somehow believed they were a threat to them or society. Neither the local media nor the police were able to slow the growth of punk rock.

It started in Newport Beach with the local PD pulling over kids. They would profile anyone with crazy haircuts, punk rock t-shirts, earrings, etc., and take photos of them to add to a binder. If there was a crime committed, they would pull out the binder and let people go through the photos of the punks in the book. With the success of this catching and identifying what they considered to be low-level criminals, Huntington Beach followed suit and adopted the same procedure by starting a binder of their own. This profiling of punks is what we called, "Punk in Public." Whether you were riding a bike, skateboarding, or walking around, they would pull you over, take your picture, and add it to the book.

One time the police parked in front of my apartment for a call they had about a party that was happening around the corner. Instead, they decided to come to my door and proceeded to make everyone inside go outside on the sidewalk, took Polaroids of them, and gathered information on everyone at my party. They threatened to arrest me which was the only reason everyone went outside in the first place. This treatment of punks only ended when the police pulled it on a kid whose father was a high-powered lawyer in Newport Beach. They settled out of court, and the book was never brought out again. It seems the punk binders just disappeared.

EARLY PUNK ROCK IN HB & LB

In the beginning, Huntington Beach didn't seem to have many of us punks; you could count on two hands, our population. But there were more of us out there, and punk seemed to be spreading like wildfire. We would begin to see more and more punks show up at house parties, warehouses, and garages, wherever we could play music. We weren't the first punks in HB or the surrounding areas, but we were pretty early on the scene. The Orange County scene, and specifically in HB was quite different compared to the Hollywood scene. We had a surf day-glo kind of thing in the beginning, going on, all credit to the original surf punks, a band called The Crowd. Jim Decker, Jay Decker, James Kaa, and Barry Cuda had a style collected from thrift store finds, DIY outfits, and the vibe at the beach. The Crowd was the most prolific band in my mind.

Steve Reehl of The Hated, in my mind, was one of the first crossover surf punks I ever met. This was well before punk even existed, in the mid-70s, when I was just a young kid hanging out. I noticed his style, his attitude, his haircuts, and his fucking mouth! I'll talk more about Steve in the next chapter, and how he influenced me in my early surfing years.

A bunch of other bands came out of HB; China White, The Screws, The Slashers, The Outsiders, and The Klan, etc. I think The Slashers originally played Sex Pistols cover if I remember correctly. Very early on, these bands were all playing house parties. My first real show at a venue in HB was at the Golden Bear, which has been closed since 1986, it was to see The Dickies and The Weirdos. We were pogoing, as slam dancing didn't exist yet, nonetheless bouncing straight up and down scared the security. They freaked out and started throwing us around like rag dolls and beating us up. The adrenaline and the excitement of the whole thing was amazing.

Again, I can't say enough about The Crowd and the giant influence they were if you were from Huntington Beach. They were power pop punk and had an image and energy completely different from anyone else at the time. It was nothing like the English / NYC vibe or the LA scene. The leather studs and spikes, bondage gear, crazy colored hair, and leather jackets that were the style at that time, we couldn't afford. Later it seemed to become the norm for punk rock.

Ron used to skateboard, so this brought us together with a lot of other punks. Ron went to Fullerton and stayed a few days with some of these guys who would later become the Adolescents, the true kids of the black hole. They took him to an abandoned graveyard on the side of a hill where the bones were just falling out of the graves. They had some of these bones in their studio, and we thought it was just crazy. To my knowledge, this was the first time Ron tried heroin, as these guys were already experimenting with it.

Many bands were to emerge out of Fullerton. Middle Class, formed in '76 and released an EP, *Out of Vogue* in '78, they were generally considered one of the first bands to play hardcore punk. They were a favorite of ours. Also, from Fullerton were Social Distortion, Agent Orange, and later Christian Death. We were a small part of something much bigger that was happening. Things were starting to change. At least in our world, music became wide open, and a new vibe, sound, and feel were all around us. If you had a guitar or bass, you could start a band, or maybe just the will or want to do it was enough. There were plenty of bands that came out with no musical background or equipment. It was new and exciting and there were no rules; at least none that we obeyed. We didn't know any better.

Skating at an unfinished skate park somewhere near Long Beach, Ron met, who would later become the guys in Vicious Circle, Todd, Pat, Pasta, Bill R, Scott B, Pat Brown (RIP), and Mr. Wilson were among some of the early crew. Pat was riding a moped, going vertical down the snake run at this unfinished and too rough to skate, under-construction skate park that they probably broke into. Ron came home and said, "I met eight punks in Long Beach." We were ecstatic. My only contact with Vicious

Circle, prior to that, was in the pit at the Cuckoo's Nest with Rick Bressie, aka Pasta (RIP) when he and I almost got into a fight in the pit. We were soon to be thick as thieves. There were so few punks at the time, so to go anywhere and meet other punks was a sign that we were starting to grow in numbers.

I remember there was a contest at Big O skate park in Orange. We were in the parking lot hanging out, probably smoking and drinking beer. Skate competitions for the youth were like a lot of other sports with the parents there to support their kids. Duane Peters was there; he was still pretty new to punk, but he was hanging out in the parking lot partying with us. They called out his name for the heat which was problematic because he was standing with us and so he had to skate across the parking lot through the crowds of people at the gate and drop straight into the pool as his heat had already started and the clock was running. He somehow landed it at the bottom, which I think later became one of his signature tricks, maybe called an Acid drop, but it was gnarly. Duane was crazy good and probably won the contest, but I don't remember.

Back in the parking lot, things had taken a turn for the worse. It seemed the "milk and cookie" parents of some of the younger skaters had taken exception to us partying in the parking lot. There was a small crowd developing by now telling us to leave. Funny thing is, one of the younger guys with these parents was George, who later became the drummer of Christian Death. I guess he hadn't found his punk rock roots yet. We were, once again, kicked out of a public place; probably more for looks than our behavior. It was just another normal day of early punk in Orange County.

The aftermath of the morning news report at Infinity resulted in my less-than-graceful exit from Huntington Beach. Losing my job and apartment, I ended up living at Todd's studio behind his house in Long Beach, Ron soon followed. There were couches in the studio and a bunch of stolen equipment. We started rehearsing together, trying to start a new band. We were a three-piece; just Todd, Ron, and myself. We began writing songs that, some of which, would later become the first EP. Our days were spent sleeping off hangovers and trying to find booze and something to eat. Sometimes with a dollar in our pocket, we would enter a grocery store and buy bread which, at the time, you could get for forty cents. We managed to steal packaged sandwich meat and cheese and whatever else we could stuff in our combat boots or pockets. We were starving. Our nights were spent finding more beer and practicing with an occasional party or show to follow.

As always, the usual suspects would begin to show up back at Todd's. The whole Long Beach crew cycled through our place on a daily basis. Pat Brown, Scott Burson, Rick Bressi, Paul Weber, Mr. Wilson (Tom Wilson), and Bill Richards among the many others. Todd lived with his grandparents who, given their age, put up with a lot of shit. He was a misbehaving handful. On one occasion Bob, Todd's grandfather, came outside and noticed that there were tombstones in the studio. He asked Todd, "What is this, what are you doing, where did you get these?" Todd yelled back, "I picked them up, old man." His grandfather was visibly upset and said to get rid of them. So, we did, by burying them in the backyard. These, along with many other things that needed to go away, are buried in that yard. There was a constant parade of stolen equipment, guitars, amps, and mixing boards, most of which we didn't even know how to use, and all of which were of questionable origin.

THE BEGINNING OF TSOL

The first song I learned how to play was, "Somethin' Else" by Eddie Cochran, made famous by Sid, depending on where you stand. In the beginning, I had only taken one music lesson, and at the time that seemed like enough. In some way, it was great being so blind to the normal way things were done. This allowed me to have no walls, no barriers, and no rules; and sometimes it even worked. I didn't know anything about a verse or a chorus, and I didn't care. It was about attitude, anger, and wanting to be heard. It was about being in a band. The truth is that later on I would want to learn more about the craft I had chosen, and I did take some lessons to try and learn how to read music. That was contrary to what I believed because I didn't want to play anybody else's music. I'm basically unschooled and play by ear.

We didn't want anything to do with anyone who had come before us, meaning the rock establishment and the rules that confined them. We didn't have a clue what we were doing really, but we were doing it like so many others at the time. Making music up and down the coast and all over the nation; writing songs in garages, basements, bedrooms, or an attic. Wherever you could find a place to put padding on the walls and get away with playing too loud or poorly, we would play.

The name TSOL was a holdover from 14th and Olive during a late-night drinking and drugging session. We were watching a religious show, and it had a band or a choir called "The Sounds of Liberty." Pat, me, or somebody in the room yelled out that we should have a band called the True Sounds of Liberty! Pat was the first one to run out of the apartment yelling, **TSOL, TSOL!** I had no idea why he was yelling that. I hadn't put it together yet, but it stuck.

While we were all living at Todd's, one day in the backyard, Todd was playing Viking while chopping something in half with a sword he had fabricated and creating mayhem. At some point, we noticed two skinny, young punks standing at the backyard gate. Pat approached them as we watched from a distance. A quiet conversation took place. Then they stood there nervously, as Pat walked back toward us. When he got close, I asked, "Who is that?" Pat replied, "We stole their drum kit, and they would like it back." I said, "Well?" Todd just stood there, shrugged his shoulders, and didn't seem to care. I told Todd, "They have balls for coming here, give it back to them." Todd said, "OK." They were Humann, the bassist, and Joey Escalante, the drummer of The Vandals. This kind of chaos was normal. There never seemed to be any problems or issues; it was just daily life for us. You will see a thread develop of this kind of thinking that permeated our lifestyles.

While living at Todd's was fun on many levels, learning how to play with Todd and Ron as a group and making as much noise as we wanted, whenever we wanted, was priceless! We were living with little or no responsibility; no bills to pay and sleeping off hangovers all day just to wake up and do it all over again. Did I mention no responsibility? This also meant sleeping on dirty couches in a dirty well-used practice/party room with graffitied walls and beer-barf-soaked carpet. We had no money and zero food, which was pretty low on our radar as long as we had beer. Somebody always seemed to show up willing to contribute or to make a beer run, but I think Ron and I were actually starving.

At this point, we had played as a three-piece once or maybe even twice at Jerry Roach's the Cuckoo's Nest in Costa Mesa. I think we did pretty well, but something was missing. We needed a frontman if we really wanted to kick it into high gear. There were a few names mentioned; Steve Olson, friend and pro skater, was in the running, and we even tried out, playing a house party, with a guy named Rick who had bad habits. We needed somebody bigger than life; someone with an undeniable presence.

I always remembered Jack Grisham from parties and shows where we were, but he seemed to appear and then just disappear. There seemed to be a light about him; always grinning and smiling and seemed pretty much bulletproof. He was always dressed way over the top, and a bit aloof, but possibly hiding a dark side, like a modern-day Jack the Ripper persona, somewhat mysterious. He was completely different from anyone else. He was charismatic and seemed to hold people's attention.

Jack had a band for a bit, Vicious Circle, in which Todd was the drummer, Laddie played bass, and Steve Houston, I believe, on guitar. The Vicious Circle crew was the center of every show. One night there was a giant fight with Jack kicking somebody in the audience in the head. After a while, that guy returned with a gun. Although I wasn't there, to my knowledge, that guy didn't actually shoot anyone, but after that, Jack understandably retired from punk rock for a little while. He spent some time in Alaska cooling off, literally.

Sooner rather than later, Jack returned, and I would see him at shows in the oddest places. At times it would seem like I saw him everywhere I went, making eye contact, but he was always leaving before we could connect. One night at a club in LA, we glanced at each other across a crowd of people and nodded. We both looked down at the ground at the same time and noticed a wallet, which we both dove for; we came back up, each of us holding onto it. Jack took the wallet, opened it up, pulled out two twenty-dollar bills, tossed the wallet away, and promptly tore the two bills in half, putting half in his pocket and giving the other half to me. At the time it seemed completely normal except when I realized, a few days later, I couldn't spend two halves of two different twenties. Again, it's just the way we thought. It took me weeks to find Jack and get back the other half of my twenty-dollar bill.

Ron and I walked a few blocks from Todd's to Jack's house to ask him if he wanted to join the band. His mother answered the door, and we asked her if Jack was home. Jack came to the door, we made our pitch to him, and he was receptive. We later learned that his mom had said something to him before he came to the door like, "Who are these boys, be careful, what do they want from you?" I'm guessing we didn't make a great impression on his mother. As luck or fate would have it, Jack became our singer, and the rest is history. Jack's escapades are that of legend; he was and is larger than life. Mrs. Grisham was supporting, loving, tolerant, and kind; at times Jack's house felt like a second home to me.

Jack began to come over to the studio to rehearse and write. We had written most of the songs that would be on our first EP prior to Jack joining, but he was able to contribute and put his fingerprint on what would later become the first EP, The Black Record. With the band in place, and Jack as our singer, we started playing more garages, backyards, parking lots, baseball diamonds, and anywhere you could plug in an amp. We played until we were run off and would head to the next spot that had power.

The Cuckoo's Nest was quickly becoming a stronghold of ours. I don't remember how many people it held but seemed to be a couple hundred at best and we were selling out. TSOL's first real show was there on September 3, 1980, opening for The Descendants and Bible Burners. Shows and records followed fast and furiously, as we were out to make a name for ourselves. We played the Cuckoo's Nest three more times before the end of the year, and we were headlining by December. As we headed into the early 80s our local shows were pretty big and loaded with great bands that were of punk rock legend.

Finding venues to play wasn't always easy due to punk rock's reputation, so outside of backyard parties and parking lots, the Cuckoo's Nest was the only consistent club in So Cal to play. It was next door to a country bar called Zoobies which made for plenty of excitement. There was constant conflict between the Zoobies patrons and the punks. The seemingly childish aspect of this was also dangerous and possibly criminal. These were grown men picking fights with the punks, basically kids and teenagers. The controversy over the scene, style of dancing, and music resulted in a constant battle with the City of Costa Mesa. As much as Jerry Roach tried to please the powers that be, ultimately The Cuckoo's Nest was shut down. Jerry fought for us and made it personal by fighting for our First Amendment rights. He was quoted as saying, "I wanted to shove punk rock up their asses." If it wasn't for Jerry giving the scene an outlet and the platform for us to play, the punk rock scene in Orange

County would've ended up in a very different place. I have a lot of respect for Jerry Roach.

Someone else needs to be mentioned, Ed Colver, who was a friend, fan, and brilliant photographer. He was early on the scene, supporting the bands, and taking photos. He was seemingly at every show capturing and chronicling the whole movement. Without his contribution and the historical importance of his photographs, there would be no visual history of a once-in-a-lifetime musical movement.

Our fan base started to grow, as did our reputation. The shows started getting bigger and wilder. We went from small clubs to playing halls, then theaters with thousands of kids. We still weren't making much money. Early on we had recorded a demo in Westminster, CA, and sold one of Ron's cabinets to pay for it. I think we got about two hundred dollars for it, as I remember. The recording wasn't very good.

By now it was 1980 and we had played San Diego, which was a complete debacle the first time. One of our crew or hang-arounds got into a dispute with one of the locals and it turned into a stand-off where we had to leave the club before it got any worse. Next, it was on to San Francisco, must've been at Mabuhay Gardens on Broadway, Dirk Dirksen's club. He was a music promoter in the late 70s and early 80s and he was called the *Pope of Punk*. We were staying up the street at Sammy Wong's, a place at the edge of Chinatown where we liked to stay. It couldn't have been more than twenty dollars a room. It was close to the clubs and cheap. That's when we received the first contract from Posh Boy. I don't remember how it got into our hands, but it was promptly and literally flushed down the toilet, clogging the plumbing and pissing off both Posh Boy and the hotel.

It would be on or around May 1981 when we signed with Posh Boy, Robbie Fields, and released our first EP. We needed a record out if we wanted to continue moving up the ranks, gaining more fans, and playing bigger shows. The first EP was our older songs. We had already written songs for *Dance With Me* but chose to give Posh Boy the older songs for the EP since we didn't really trust him.

We were a much better band with Jack singing than we ever would've been with just me and Ron. We were a band now with a crew, friends, and even fans. Our lives were all about playing shows, practicing, partying, drinking, and hanging out with our crew.

We had a big show coming up with DOA and the Red Rockers at the Vex but realized our equipment was not up to par. We needed to upgrade, so it was decided the boys would "go shopping" at a new music store in Santa Ana with no bars on the windows. This was problematic because the store was on a main street, downtown, near the police station. So, a plan was made, the time was set, and off they went. The boys pulled up in front of the store, and Pat got out of the car and ran up to the window with a golf club! He hit it which caused the window to flex horribly, and he was pulled back thinking he would end up a bloody casualty from the shattered glass. Next, something bigger was used to break through the window and it came crashing down. Pat immediately ran inside and emerged minutes later with two Rickenbacher basses. They said, "No, Les Pauls!" He said, "These are for Roche." He ran straight back in to get two Les Pauls for Ron as the guys were unloading Marshals from the front window. Not exactly gone in 60 seconds, but under 5 minutes. They made it back to Long Beach unfollowed and not stopped; it was a success! Needless to say, the night of the show we had some nice-looking equipment.

During that same year, we went on to sign another bad deal that would haunt us for the next 40 years. We signed with Lisa Fantcher's Frontier Records for the *Dance with Me* album. The record took us in a completely different direction and surprised a lot of our fan base. Although we had already been playing the songs in our set prior to the release.

It was great to have labels trying to put out our records, but in hindsight, we just ended a 40-year battle to get the rights to our first two records back. So, who really won? There is no way for us to ever know the actual record sales from our first three records. We were never provided this information from Posh Boy, Frontier Records, or Alternative Tentacles. Looking back now, I'm sure there was at least a gold record in there somewhere, but sadly in our forty years as a band, we will never know. Punk rock labels didn't report to the powers that be. In addition, there's the issue of bootlegs pouring in from all over the world, and with early labels not reporting sales and no accounting of any kind, we were in the dark.

The Dance With Me album was produced by Thom Wilson (RIP) who later went on to produce Offspring's *Smash* album. Noodles and Dexter chose him because of their admiration and fondness for TSOL, particularly *Dance With Me*. Thom went on to produce albums for The Adolescents, DK, Social Distortion, The Vandals, Christian Death, and Bouncing Souls. Offspring's Smash went on to sell eleven million records worldwide. One of Offspring's first big shows was an opening slot featuring Cadillac Tramps and TSOL headlining at The Celebrity Theater. The *Dance With Me* album cover was designed by Noodle's uncle.

We first met Thom Wilson when we signed on with Frontier to do our *Dance With Me* record. Thom produced *Dance With Me*, *Weathered Statues*, and *Beneath the Shadows*. He was a real record producer with credits such as Ringo Starr, Barbra Streisand, Boz Skaggs, The Guess Who, Seals and Crofts, etc. Eventually, he would become the producer for a who's who of punk and alternative music including, The Adolescents, Dead Kennedys, Christian Death, The Vandals, Social Distortion, Bad Religion, Bouncing Souls, and The Offspring. Thom was low-key funny and a friendly guy who got it, not trying to change us, but rather just record us and insert ideas when and where he could.

During this time, I crossed paths, again, with Steve Reehl. Back in the day, he really just put up with kids like me and hardly paid us any attention. So, when Steve reached out to me about a potential job at a surf shop in HB, I was more than interested and it was something I had to do. After all, I had lost my job at Infinity and was starving. I couldn't find a pair of jeans without holes in the knees to wear to the interview, but I put on a white dress shirt and headed down to meet Abdul and Steve at Sunline.

The interview seemed to go well, after all, I did know how to work at and even run a surf shop. It was a little weird having Abdul's older brother, a doctor overseas, as he was unable to practice in the States watch our every move. In the beginning, he wouldn't even let us ring up sales. This eventually eased up, as he began to trust us. The truth is, we turned a business that was sure to fail into a total success. When he bought the shop, he basically bought the name. There was little or no inventory and HB was pretty localized, to say the least. That's the nicest way I can explain what Abdul, or any new breed of foreign shop owners, thought of downtown at the time. Steve and I worked as a buffer, if you will, with the connections in the surf industry and the locals downtown.

Steve ended up moving on, and I became the manager. Eventually, I was able to get an apartment on Alabama Street back in HB. I shared a two-bedroom with Brock Stussy at that time whose brother went on to become a famous fashion designer who started as a surf wear company. Sadly, Brock drowned when he jumped off the HB pier with a friend, both on PCP, emulating the Blues Brothers. The water was too shallow, and it knocked him out so hard that he drowned. His friend survived and ran home soaking wet completely unaware of what had just happened to his buddy. (RIP Brock)

Sometimes it's not so much about making a mark on the world. It could be it was enough to have influenced someone with a song, a sound, an attitude, or an idea greater than yours. — M.R.

GOLDENVOICE

The biggest shows were always put on by Goldenvoice's Gary Tover and Paul Tollett. I can't say enough about how important Gary and Paul were to the scene. If it weren't for Goldenvoice, there would've never been big shows or the scene, as we know it. They even paid the bands their guarantees, and that didn't happen often back in the beginning. Goldenvoice made it possible for punk rock to grow and flourish.

On December 4, 1981, we did our first show for Gary Tovar and what was to become, Goldenvoice Productions. It was at La Casa de la Raza, a Community Center since the 1970s in Santa Barbara California. We played with Shattered Faith and Rhino 39. I don't remember anything about the show except that we were there playing for Gary. I don't even recall how many times we had met before. My point is that Gary and Paul became the architects of the big shows. They successfully promoted bigger and bigger shows at better venues. In the beginning, Gary financed his love of punk rock shows by selling weed, lots of weed. The harder the police, city, or government tried to shut him down, the harder he pushed back. Despite the city fines, he continued to put on punk shows. At one point they stationed police inside the club, citing that he didn't have a "Dance" permit. So, anytime anyone jumped up and down, they would write another ticket. He was in and out of court constantly with hundreds of citations all with fines attached.

Our EP was released in May of '81 on Poshboy Records, which was quickly followed by the *Dance With Me* LP, released in June on Frontier Records. We did close to one hundred shows in 1981 including a 20-date national tour supporting the *Dance with Me* release. We went on to release *Weathered Statues* in early '82 before adding Greg Kuehn to the band that summer. *Beneath the Shadows* followed later the same year. Both were released on Alternative Tentacles.

We were looking to add a keyboard player, as we were starting to grow musically, and wanted to experiment. I believe it was Jack's idea to add keys. This added more dimension to what we already had. Opening us up to so many different sounds at the flip of a switch; piano, synthesizers, horns, etc. Mike Brown, "Cheeseboy," a friend of ours who later became the manager for Sublime with Rome, introduced Greg to us. Mike knew that Greg was a fan who happened to play keyboards. Greg went to school with the brother of Gil, the bouncer at The Cuckoo's Nest, who was in a band with Alfie Agnew. Having an in at the Cuckoo's Nest, he had seen us play on Tuesday night bills. Greg was still in high school at the time and describes our early shows like a shark frenzy. As many punk bands as he saw there, he recalls the power behind our music and the response of the crowd was nothing like he'd ever seen before.

Following our introduction, we had an impromptu meeting at his parent's house. He had a studio set up with equipment and songbooks lying around; little did he know, it was his audition. Jack picked up an Elton John book and asked Greg if he could play something. So, he did, it could've been Tiny Dancer, but that was it and he was in. Jack asked him to come down and play with us at the studio set up in his garage in Long Beach. That's when TSOL became a five-piece.

Greg had played with bands before, but never with anyone like us. It was a learning experience for him to figure out where to fit in as a keyboard player with Todd and myself. We had a great trajectory going and adding Greg on keyboards took us to the next level. He had bits and pieces of music he had written on cassette which would later become *Beneath The Shadows* and Soft Focus. We were always forward thinking; wanting to become broader and different, and there was a certain appeal to be part of it all. Greg was attending CSLB on a full scholarship as a classic piano major at the time. He gave up school to be in TSOL. All things considered, his parents took the news very well. Our manager, Mike Varaney did pay a visit to talk with his parents about the plan to record and go on tour, and that seemed to be enough for them to support Greg joining the band.

The Galaxy was the first show Greg played with us. The amount of equipment he had to haul around was crazy. The piano, synthesizer, organ, Yamaha keyboard, and whatever else couldn't have been the easiest part of playing. It's amazing today to see the progression of equipment and what can be done with minimal gear. That is if you're Greg Kuehn.

We played with a truly crazy array of bands from Black Flag to Bauhaus. Live shows were and are the lifeblood of our music, at least, I believe they were and still are to me. The early shows were insane, from the giant interlocking circle pits to kids jumping from second-story balconies, grabbing curtains, sliding down to the PA stacks, 20 feet off the ground then jumping into the pit. Unbelievable and crazy sights like this were quite common. We viewed this as normal, as it was getting harder to shock us, and after all, shock value was a currency of sorts.

There were shows at the Hollywood Palladium, The Olympic Auditorium, Santa Monica Civic Center, The Vex, as well as big warehouses and off-the-wall clubs. Thousands of punks were turning up at the bigger shows and we were right there in the middle of a big storm, if you will. It seemed as if nothing could touch us. We always seemed to get in and out of wherever we were at just the right time. Whether it was a fight breaking out or the Riot Police, who frequently showed up to practice their techniques at shows, or it seemed. We somehow drove in to watch a show, participate in the chaos, and then walk, run, or sometimes drive away unscathed. It was an electric time in So Cal and for So Cal music, especially punk. On any given night, something was happening; be it a house party, warehouse party, or a club.

We were a band, a crew, and even a gang to some. As a band, we were satellites spinning together, yet separately and completely out of control at times. We would come together, and sparks would fly; we had a beautifully toxic chemistry that made us an explosive unit. We had different ideas and different identities with a similar goal, thread, or even rope that loosely bound us together; that is if chaos and destruction are considered goals. The best part and sometimes the problem was we didn't care. We all had our part and with Jack as the always-charismatic ringmaster, and at times, psychotic leader; the sky was the limit.

We liked playing, writing, and recording songs. The shows were everything and music was just a vehicle to get there. But, as for the business side of the industry, we had no clue where to begin and seemingly didn't care to learn, so we wrote and played. We felt like we were the first generation that adopted the battle cry of Destroy. This wasn't our idea, of course, it came from the Sex Pistols, but it sounded like a good idea to us. We believed in it completely, which probably had something to do with our bad business decisions and the way we lived our daily lives; scorched earth seemed to be our way. I don't think we were looking for much of a future. Everything we did seemed to be complete for the moment.

At some point, some of our peers seemed to figure out the business and learned how to play the game. Whether it was with existing record labels or even creating their own label, marketing distribution, royalties, and learning the business side of things, some had it down. We never really got it, not for years and not until everything was gone or taken from us. Whatever punk is or isn't, was or wasn't, we were never in it for money, fame, or glory.

EARLY SHOWS & TOURING

During the early days, we had to really sell it at every show. We had to prove ourselves every night and in every town. Most of the towns had their own ideas of who and what they thought was cool. Even if they were the least bit familiar with us, there was a known distance, so to speak. We usually had to win the crowd over and prove ourselves again and again. This became more evident the farther from home we were. Riverside was harder than LA, San Diego was even harder, and so on and so on.

Needless to say, heading to another state was ten times harder, and the East Coast was a whole other world. If we weren't being hassled at the truck stops on the interstate in the middle of nowhere, stopped by the police, harassed by jocks, construction workers, or cowboys, or just not being served at the local restaurants, we certainly dealt with it at our shows. Most bigger cities had their own bands, gangs, and scene already established. I felt we had an edge in bigger cities with more people; that they were, at least, a bit more likely to have heard of us. My point is this shit was not easy. In all fairness, we received this same treatment at home early on in good old Huntington Beach.

In the weeks leading up to the Beneath the Shadows tour, we had an opportunity to play with Bauhaus in San Francisco at the Old Waldorf on Battery Street. The club opened in 1976 and has hosted some of the biggest names in music history such as AC/DC, Dire Straits, Blue Oyster Cult, Iggy Pop, Blondie, Metallica, Pat Benatar, REM, Gary Moore, U2, and Dead Kennedys. On this night, it was Bauhaus with TSOL as direct support.

As familiar as we were to San Francisco, and being that it was home to our management, soundman, and crew, this venue had never previously allowed us to play there. Although we had played The Old Fillmore, Mabuhay Gardens on Broadway, and others; until the Beneath the

Shadows album, neither we nor our fan base had not been deemed a good fit for such a high-end venue. This was a big deal of sorts, as we were fans of Bauhaus. This was a beautiful club with a cool outside area.

We loaded in that afternoon and Bauhaus' crew was halfway through setting up the stage with equipment and lights. As we waited, it seemed as if they were really taking their time. After all, they were the headliner, so they decided to take a long lunch break. When they finished doing what they needed to do, they finally continued setting up. It was getting late, so any thought of a soundcheck for us was out the door. Bauhaus' crew had positioned cool floor lighting surrounding each band member made for a dark, dramatic stage presence. Although no room for movement, seemingly each band member must have stayed in place, except for Peter Murphy.

It was getting late, and doors were ready to open when the road crew told us to set up along the front of the stage. The problem was, we had only a couple of feet of unused space with which to work. Pretty impossible to set up keyboards, drums, and bass. We complained that we didn't have enough room to set up, and they seemed totally uninterested with our problems. So, after speaking with our manager, we decided to tell them we were going to leave. At that point, they decided they were willing to move some of the mood lighting which allowed us a whole three feet across the front of the stage. This was still completely unacceptable to us. We would have to set up and play in a straight line across the front of the stage, each member side by side, which we had never done. They weren't willing to budge, but at that point, our manager, Mike Varaney, talked us off a cliff, and we decided to move forward and just play under those circumstances.

I don't remember how good or bad the show sounded, but we gave it our all and soldiered through despite how uncomfortable and strange it was. That stage configuration would be the first and last time we ever played in that arrangement in all our 40 years. After that show, Bauhaus had lost a little of their appeal to me.

On another early tour, we were sent out with Microwave, a Dead Kennedys crew member that Mike and Cindy had loaned to us.

Microwave was a smart capable tour manager, driver, and roadie; a real fix it and get it done kind of guy. The problem was, he was used to the DKs who behaved like adults, for the most part. We on the other hand were, at this point, no better than a bunch of animals. Juvenal delinquents unwilling to have our daily misbehaving controlled or managed in any way. It also didn't help that we weren't really making any money. It was pretty much a starvation tour. When it came down to whether to drink or eat, the answer was always drink, and then figure out the rest later. Microwave had his hands full, to say the least.

We were sort of modern-day pirates, trying to come home from tour with plunder or booty. In fact, on the next tour, Microwave kept us outside of the towns where we were playing by having us sleep at truck stops and rest areas in the vehicle, due to how much trouble we caused if allowed to be in a town unchecked with access to alcohol. When we arrived anywhere, we scattered like starving rats off a sinking ship. All or most of us were a potential small-scale crime wave at the very least. We were always at risk of doing something stupid that might cause us to miss the show that night. I won't mention who the worst offenders were, but the threat and risk were quite real. Usually, it was just alcohol we were after, but it could also be anything that wasn't nailed down; gear or other things lying around in the club or hall, a lonely pinball machine meets screwdriver was a favorite of some.

The first time playing Tucson was pretty interesting. Just in how different things could be from state to state, and how sheltered we really were in some ways. When we arrived at the bar where we were playing that night, I jumped out of the vehicle to check it out. I headed into the bright sunlight and heat of the day to the entrance of the club, a bar really, and pushed the door open. As my eyes adjusted to the light, I saw biker guys who looked more like prospectors straight out of a western cowboy movie. They were playing pool, sitting at the bar drinking, and standing around. All or most glanced my way as I opened the door and every one of them had a sidearm in a holster on their hip. I, on the other hand, was dressed in black pegged jeans, a cut-away t-shirt, a leather jacket, army boots, and spiked hair. I walked back outside to jokingly tell the guys,

"Wait till you see this, you're going to love it!" We weren't in Kansas anymore.

In July of '81, we played a festival, Eastern Front at The Aquatic Park in Berkley. We were third on the bill beneath Flipper and DOA. The entire lineup consisted of; DOA, Flipper, TSOL, The Lewd, War Zone, The Fix, 7 Seconds, Sic Pleasure, Anti–L.A., The Slits, Snakefinger, The Offs, Earl Zero, Middle Class, The Wounds, Toiling Midgets, and Tanks. It was giant and a really big deal for us!

At some point during the show, I met a beautiful girl, but forgot to get her phone number or did and lost it. I remembered she told me she worked at the California Mart in LA. When I got home from San Francisco I decided I would try to find her, so I bribed a friend to drive me there. Upon entering the building, I realized I was fucked. The place was giant, at least twenty stories with more than one street entrance. I walked around looking in showrooms, floor after floor, with no luck. So, I headed downstairs to the café with my friend to have a couple of beers. As luck would have it, I knew the guy working in the café, Bernie Bernstein. He was in a band, and I knew him from the scene. We said hi and he asked what I was doing there. I explained who I was looking for, and he told me that she worked on the 11th floor. We finished our beers and headed back upstairs. Sure enough, there she was, and I imagine excited to see me, as she came back to HB with me that afternoon and became my girlfriend. We had a whirlwind of a relationship only to be made more complicated by the amount of touring the band was doing.

During this time the original TSOL was heavily touring. Needless to say, things worsened on the home front. One particular tour had ended, and I flew into LAX expecting to be picked up by my girlfriend. Upon arrival, I was torn up, shabby at best, carrying an anvil case with my black T Bird bass in it and a small suitcase. I was exhausted and falling asleep on a bench while waiting for the ride that never came. I gave a homeless guy ten dollars to watch me and my stuff while I dosed off. When she never showed, I called a close friend of mine, Freddy, to come pick me up. When Freddy arrived, he had some coke so I promptly woke up as we headed back to HB.

Back at his house, I was still unable to reach my girlfriend, so I borrowed his Yamaha scooter and went to my apartment. Once there, I had no way to get in because my girlfriend still had the keys. I used an old trick that usually worked when I was locked out by gently pushing on the glass while trying to open the latch and CRACK! The window shattered, and I cut the top of my hand. That was bad enough, but I also had a piece of glass sticking out of my wrist. I pulled the glass out which made things worse and by now I was bleeding heavily. I took off my leather jacket and t-shirt trying to stop the bleeding, I wrapped it around my wound and jumped on the Yamaha, using my left hand on the throttle, and headed down to Pacifica Hospital. Luckily, it was just down the street and my mom had worked there for years. I arrived looking like a fucking mess. Bloody and dirty, dressed in leather pants with a t-shirt soaked in blood, I was a wreck. I guess that's what they thought too because the cops were the next to arrive. I was stitched up, but not allowed to leave until the cops had a look at my apartment and the scene of the crime, or rather my stupidity. Fred picked me up from the hospital with some other guy who rode the scooter home.

Things only got better from there. As I went around trying to collect on drug debts that were owed to me (yes, I sold coke and weed from time to time), I soon found out my girlfriend and her new boy toy, Eddie, had gone around and collected all cash owed to me while I was away. As if it couldn't get any worse, the new boy toy would later become the keyboard player in Jack and Greg's new band, Cathedral of Tears. I always thought Eddie liked guys. I guess he was into girls after all.

Things came to a head a few nights later when I went to my old friend Jesse's house. Jesse referred to his house as "The Paisley." I had known Jesse (RIP) and his brother James for years. James played bass in China White. I found out my ex-girlfriend was there partying, so I borrowed Freddy's scooter and headed over to the house alone, but she wouldn't come out of the room once I arrived. Shortly after, I was escorted outside by five or six guys. I was fresh off tour, tired, and broken with my hand stitched up and arm in a sling. I was in no condition to fight anyone; I was down hundreds of dollars and pretty beat up. Despite this, I must've looked pretty intimidating because I ended up surrounded by a bunch of guys in the front yard. In my mind, this wasn't going to end well for me. I reached into my pocket and pulled out my pearl-handled switchblade, "Click." Immediately the circle that had formed around me magically disappeared, so I left.

I went home to lick my wounds and to see what was next in store for me. I don't remember how much later this happened, but late one night I was at a girl's apartment near my place. She lived above Villa Sweden on Main St. We were doing coke and drinking with a few people when the girl I was hanging out with told me Mike Ness was in one of the bedrooms dope sick and twenty dollars would get him well. I thought, well, that's crazy so I gave her twenty dollars.

This seemed like a small thing since I had money and a job, so she took the twenty and disappeared. I don't remember who left or how long they were gone, but sometime later Mike appeared with a small piece of plastic in his hand. He said something to the effect of, "Here's your half." I said, "No, just keep it, it's yours." He insisted it was my half, so I took it. I had never done it before and was a little scared of even trying it and honestly didn't know how. I knew you could smoke it or shoot it, but I'd never tried heroin. I mostly did coke, speed, smoked weed, and drank. But I put it in the coin pocket of my Levi's and didn't think much about it. Later that night or into the early morning he was feeling a lot better. We weren't close friends, but I knew him from the scene. We talked a little, but at the time, different bands from different scenes acted a little like rival gangs.

Mike turned out to be a smart leader who survived his checkered past of the early days. He and his band, Social Distortion fought in the trenches for new music among a sea of bands at the time. Today he still fronts Social Distortion, one of the biggest bands to come out of the Orange County punk rock scene. I don't really need to say much about his accomplishments, he is and was the real deal.

After cutting my hand and the debacle with my ex at the apartment, I was feeling low and needed something different, some other form of relief. Remembering what I had on the top shelf, I thought it might help.

So, I got a piece of foil, put the tar on top, and cautiously tried to smoke it, otherwise known as *chasing the dragon*. I thought it sounded kind of cool. I didn't know how to do it correctly, this being the first time, so I put a little piece onto the tinfoil and inhaled the smoke. I was still scared of it, but it began to ease the pain a little. I never gave this much thought until recently, but it would be the first time I tried heroin. Just another brick in the wall.

SOMEWHERE IN MIDDLE AMERICA

The tour started with the first show in Long Beach at El Dorado Ram Shack. A rec center at a local park where anybody could rent the place for a party or family reunion. Bad Religion was opening for us. We had promoted the show ourselves in the hopes of making enough money to start the tour. Following the show, in the parking lot, Todd asked Humann (Steve Pfauter R.I.P.), bassist for the Vandals, if he wanted to come on tour as a roadie. With only the clothes on his back, he accepted the invitation and hopped into the motorhome, and off we went. With our managers, Mike and Cindy Vraney at the helm, this was "The Beneath the Shadows" tour.

We were pretty much unmanageable, not so much as a band, but as people, we misbehaved constantly. Each of us had our own little idiosyncrasies. The first tour was plagued by a couple of our member's compulsion to steal something every night, or rather at every club we played. Everything from booze to money; robbing coin machines, pinball machines, equipment, drum gear, P.A. stuff, mics; so much so that returning dates were in question and promoters weren't interested. Getting us booked was becoming harder for our managers. It must've been a tough job, after all this was punk rock and already deemed a pain in the ass. We made it through the first couple shows, somehow, then things calmed down slightly. At least enough so we could still tour.

One night somewhere in middle of America, we pulled up to the hall we were going to play that night, which was really just an empty storefront. It was early, so we were shown where to load in and then to an empty room downstairs where we were able to hang out. As we sat down in the basement, goofing around, and wasting time, we noticed a hole in the wall under the stairs. There were a few bricks missing and there was a scary dark space inside this hundred-year-old building. We clowned each other and naturally challenged Humann to put his hand in there. Great idea, right? After a little heckling, he agreed and crawled on his belly under the stairs into the space. It was dark, dirty, and certainly no place to lay down. As he inched closer to the hole in the bricks, he was finally able to get his arm inside. We immediately tried to scare him by kicking his leg and yelling. Despite our taunting, he continued to search and said, "Wait, I have something." We gathered closer, listened, and watched as he pulled his arm out holding a small dusty box. With box in hand, he sat up to open it and a small gun appeared. The four of us dove for the hole in the wall at the same time, fighting for a chance to grab another box. As we struggled to get our arms in there, more boxes were being pulled from the hole. There were over twenty handguns in all different shapes and styles.

Now the question remained, what are we supposed to do with them? Todd wanted to take them home, which was insane but also seemed quite normal for us at the time. He wanted to put them in the motorhome and use my bass case to transport them. Unbeknownst to Mike and Cindy, they were brought onto the motorhome that we were touring in and stashed somewhere in the back. The next morning before we left town, Todd and Humann boxed and shipped them back to LB to Todd's house. We had no idea if they would be there when the tour was over, but at least they were gone and temporarily forgotten.

In the next town we played, the promoter ended up stiffing us after a light turnout at our show. He told us to wait while he went to get the money, but he never returned. Being on a schedule, we had to leave immediately. So, although completely illegal, but totally logical to us, we took the microphones that had some value and told the sound man that when the promotor wired us our money, we would return the equipment. As we headed down the highway nearing the state line, everyone was bedded down, and we were ready for the all-night drive to the next town. Near the state line, we noticed many cars approaching with sirens and flashing lights. At the time we didn't put it together that this had anything to do with us, but we were soon stopped by the state troopers and became involved in a felony traffic stop.

Most of the road had been blocked and guns were drawn as we were ordered out of the motorhome one at a time. We were told to lay face down on the ground in the frozen dirt until everyone had exited the vehicle. While they cleared the vehicle, addressing each of us individually with guns drawn, we were ordered to stay on the ground. We were taunted with, "Hey, Faggot." "Are you a girl?" Telling us to run, "Why don't you run and see how far you get?" Adding, "You'll get a big surprise when you head over that levy." The next taunt was, "We shoot more people than they do in NYC." We assured them that we were not running and not going to cause any trouble. The situation calmed down a little, and they allowed our manager and his wife to explain why we had fled with the microphones. We were allowed to follow the Officer in Charge to the local station and address the situation. Mike, our manager, was handcuffed and rode with the officer as we followed in the motorhome. Mike later told us the officer was rubbing his leg the whole drive. When we arrived, the arresting officer walked behind his desk, put on a robe, and assumed his position of local Magistrate. He fined us with a ticket, we handed over the microphones and we were free to go. After all of this, we realized how close we really came to getting into serious trouble. All the while Mike and Cindy had no idea what could've been catastrophic had Todd not mailed the guns home. The infamous box we had happily forgotten about was right there waiting for us when we arrived back at Todd's.

The famous CBGB's in the Bowery is a former nineteenth-century saloon in NYC. The Ramones, Blondie, Talking Heads, Patti Smith, The Dead Boys, Cramps, Television, Dictators, etc. had all played that stage. To us or at least to me, it was a big deal to be there. This particular night we were doing a show with Bad Brains as the headliner and The Beastie Boys who opened for us. Ha! I had no idea who the Beastie Boys were at the time, not sure if anyone did, and I certainly had no idea who they would become.

We had played a show the night before and "somehow" the booze from the club's bar had ended up on the motorhome. Mike and Cindy were on this tour but must have been gone at the time eating or shopping because if they were around Todd would never have been able to pull it off. Here we were parked on the street in front of CBGB's. We decided to get some paper cups and start handing out drinks, shots actually. Pure booze straight out of the bottle to anyone on the street. There was a halfway house, rehab, or shelter nearby, and homeless people walking around everywhere. Just hanging out, panhandling, and waiting for the doors of the shelter to open for the night. Soon there was a line down the street all waiting for a cup of booze. Cup after cup was given out, and the street was really starting to come alive; dancing, yelling, laughing, and fighting. There was a guy on the center divider in the middle of the road, on one foot, balancing a shoe on his head; it was a real circus. That's just about the time when Mike and Cindy arrived and shut down the party. I don't think they were surprised at all at this point that we were the culprits.

We Should Be Thankful, We Don't Always Get What We Deserve. — M.R

MEETING MY MENTOR

The Pike was the center of a burnout universe. It was an amazing place along the shoreline just south of Ocean Blvd, in Long Beach. Back in the day, it was a wooden boardwalk lit by electric bulbs with dive bars, restaurants, arcades, gift shops, carnival rides, and a grand bath house. It was close to the Naval shipyards and Long Beach Harbor with fleets coming in. It attracted sailors and citizens, men and women, families, and kids all to ride the rollercoaster, see the sights, and enjoy the beach for the day. There was something to be had for everybody.

The sailors on the other hand were looking for something a little different. You could get drunk, laid, and tattooed at the very same spot families gathered on a Sunday afternoon. I imagine it was a pretty amazing place many years ago. But, in my time, the Pike was just a burned-out shell with dark streets, faded glory, and a lost luster. The only lights left on were those of tattoo shops. It was a forbidden place to go, and we loved it! The goings on there were famous in the tattoo world and far beyond.

Ron and I would go to the Pike with Todd and watch him get a new tattoo. There was a shop helper, a short biker with long hair who wore a sword on his waist that managed to bump into me every time he walked by. At the time, bikers didn't really like us at all. Punk had a negative connotation in their culture and most of them didn't understand our fashion sense or get the joke. The joke being that we weren't all gay just because we identified as punk rockers. Not that it bothered us at all that most bikers, jocks, and construction workers, at the time, thought "punk" was a gay slur. To us, it was an inside joke. The more they called us faggot, the more kisses we blew their way. Overall, there was a certain power we felt we held that just our appearance could cause such a reaction from grown men. We would hang out and browse the walls of hand-painted flash, as Ron and I had no money to get tattooed. Todd was a wild man with a gentle soul. He was a year or two younger than us, but heavily tattooed with a full-size *Eddie* from Iron Maiden on his back and Pike-style tattoos up and down his arms and legs with crass Japanese symbols for "No War" on his hand. Nobody, and I mean nobody, looked like Todd at that time. I didn't know anyone with so many tattoos, certainly no punks, although tattoos would soon be seen more and more often in our punk rock world. He got most of his tattoos by Rick Walters (RIP) at the World-Famous Pike.

Rick Walters ran Burt Grimm's tattoo parlor at the Long Beach Pike. It is the oldest tattoo shop in California; it opened in 1927. Rick became a lifelong friend and often came to shows throughout the decades. I was lucky to be able to call him a friend and work with him at Shamrock in Hollywood. One night, Ron and I had gone to get a tattoo at Bert Grimm's, but they were booked solid. Rick told us to go see a guy named Mark Mahoney at a shop the next block down toward the water called Tattoo Rose. The original Tattoo Rose sign still hangs in Mark's shop today.

We walked into The Tattoo Rose and up to the bar to watch this thin white dude tattooing some fine line black and grey on a customer. Ron and I stayed at the bar watching him tattoo and talking. He was funny and nice, and remarkably young. We noticed he had a handgun sticking out of the back of his pants. I tapped Ron and smiled, and we laughed as he finished the tattoo. He turned his chair and threw off his lap cloth which had covered his pants, and in his boot was another handgun. I quietly laughed and tapped Ron again. This was my guy, my tattooist, a master in the craft of tattooing, mentor, and lucky for me to become a life-long friend.

Mark was from Boston, but he had also lived in NYC and had tattooed there before moving to Long Beach. He had been exposed to punk rock in New York long before coming to the West Coast. After meeting Mark, we stayed in contact, and he eventually started tattooing at Jack Rudy's Tattoo Land in Anaheim. I started getting tattooed by him there and I would often just go by to hang out and visit. Tattoo shops were great back then, a complete counterculture, kind of a secret society, outlaw vibe and we loved it. Jack owned the shop and mostly showed up late at night to tattoo. Creeper was the manager, and Danny Romo and Mike Brown (RIP) rounded out the crew. Mike, Danny, and I became life-long friends.

As I mentioned before, a lot of the biker types that worked at, owned, or ran the shops didn't quite get or like punk rock or punk rockers. They mostly only tolerated us. Being from the East Coast, punk was nothing new to Mark. He had seen shows at CBGB and Max's Kansas City, as he lived, partied, and tattooed in NY. Tattooing only became legal again in NY in 1997; it had been underground before that since 1961 when a hepatitis outbreak caused tattooing to become illegal for public health and safety reasons. There were only a few early punk rock tattooists, Mad Mark Rude, Big Frank, and Joe Vegas. Johnathan Shaw wasn't really a punk but was in the middle of everything that was NYC and owned Fun City Tattoo on Saint Mark's Place in the East Village. The shop was just around the corner from Trash and Vaudeville. Tattooing was still really a secret society subculture and something you had to be invited into for the most part, and punks were still not completely accepted…not even close.

For years I followed Mark from shop to shop. From Long Beach to Anaheim to San Pedro and eventually Hollywood where he opened the first Shamrock on 3rd Street. Years later, when I got out of prison and was staying clean, Mark looked out for me. He gave me a job at Gil Montes' Tattoo Mania on the Sunset Strip in Hollywood as a helper (counter person). Tattoo Mania was a couple hundred feet from the Whisky a Go Go, a famous Hollywood institution. Gil and I, many years later, became business partners for a while. I was lucky to get to meet and know so many great tattooists. This became a turning point in my life that I'll talk more about later.

SUBURBIA

It was 1983 and three of our records were out when we were offered a performance spot in Penelope Spheeris' movie, *Suburbia*. The movie is about suburban punks who run away from home. Punk wasn't met with much understanding at this time, and this movie gave an inside look at troubled kids who refer to themselves as T.R. (The Rejected) they chose to squat in suburban abandoned tract homes rather than live with their parents. At the time, it seemed silly to us to be part of this project. We had always existed on the fringes of the music industry and probably weren't taken seriously if even acknowledged as being a valid form of music by mainstream record labels and much of the Rock press. For me personally, I didn't connect this movie to a greater understanding of the youth or our music at the time. I don't think we cared if we were understood.

We approached the whole thing with a little skepticism. We had never done anything like it before. The cast was made up of mostly non-actors at the time who later became quite famous. Future bassist for the Red Hot Chili Peppers, Flea, and Chris Pedersen, who went on to be a NASCAR driver and a well-known actor. We performed "Wash Away" and "Darker My Love". I thought it was funny when Penelope directed a couple of girls on set, who were in the Hollywood scene, to jump on stage during our song and hug Jack. We had no idea that was going to happen, and Jack was totally surprised.

To some, we were late arrivals to the party. I'm sure to the older LA punks, our behavior seemed to be ruining the punk scene, with our fan's *Clockwork Orange*-type ultraviolence in the pit; our shows could be dangerous. We were wild and reckless and a sign of the times. Each band member being over six feet tall, we were no shrinking violets. We showed up to the set pretty suspect and not taking it very seriously. It was all so different from how we normally expressed ourselves and it was almost like giving away our secret society and the inner workings of who we were. Even though it was packaged in a big birthday cake kind of fucking circus of a movie set, for us, performing and actually playing the songs was always the same, so we played it like we meant it. We played the only way we knew how, hard, mean, and serious. I think that came across in the movie.

Our scene was filmed at an old Hollywood building on Hollywood Blvd. The space was turned into a concert venue for the filming of the bands. It was crowded with extras for the movie and, I imagine, fans who just wanted to see the bands play. I had done this, myself, in the past. Once, I showed up to watch The Ramones play 30 seconds of a song, 20 times in a row, for the filming of *Rock and Roll High School* at Huntington Beach High School.

It was fun, strange, and oddly quick in many ways. The set was a lot like many venues that we had played; old, run-down, and not designed for concerts. Our usual crew showed up with us and managed to stay out of trouble for once, no fights and no thefts; quite an accomplishment for us. Normally some equipment that wasn't ours would somehow find its way into one of our vehicles, which happened more often than not.

It was comfortable having The Vandals and DI filming with us, all good songs, good bands, and good friends. Penelope was a sweetheart and seemed to get us, at least enough to put us in her movie. She had empathy for the kids and a liking for "Real Punks". She championed a cause and had earned the trust of punks following her 1981 documentary, *The Decline of Western Civilization*. A movie about the Los Angeles punk rock scene. LAPD Chief of Police Daryl Gates wrote a letter demanding that the film not be shown again in the city. I didn't know at the time, but Penelope had frequented the punk scene, checking out bands to be in her movie. Thinking back, she most likely picked us because of everything we stood for and not conforming which is exactly what *Suburbia* was about. Looking back now, I'm very grateful we were able to participate in *Suburbia* and be a part of the film.

As a rule, we responded to our perceived non-acceptance in Hollywood the only way we really knew how which wasn't very nice. We fought everything and everyone. Hollywood punks had the look, but not so much the attitude. The attitude we needed to survive was a bit more aggressive. We had to fight in Orange County, we had to fight everywhere. In fact, it was rough if you were punk. It seemed everybody had something to say, usually "Hey, Fag" or "What's up Devo?" Every construction worker, jock, cop, or long hair seemed to have a problem with us. If you were caught out alone, you could be in trouble, but in a group (a gang), things usually ended a little differently. Eventually, we started fighting back. We were an explosive, aggressive freight train flirting with self-destruction and loving every minute of it. We were like pirates with very few rules in uncharted waters. *Suburbia* really did capture aspects of how it was, isolation, loss, broken homes, prejudice, abuse, addiction, and suicide. It gave voice to a feeling that a lot of kids may have had and maybe that they were not alone.

THE BEGINNING OF THE END

1983 was the beginning of the end, certainly the beginning of the next chapter that leads up to TSOL today. But, not without many musical twists and turns, many personal changes, and in some cases, painful growth. After all, we had covered a lot of ground and put out four completely different-sounding records. In a world of new and exciting music coming from all directions, walls, barriers, and confines didn't really seem to fit or affect us. Our interests and musical tastes were different now and changing us. Each of us was drawn to something different from each other.

I believe Jack was drawn in a direction of exploration to change, shape, and shift without any one particular style. He was riding a new wave of music; New Wave, to be clear. Ron and I were digging deeper into older musical influences based on pure guitar, bass, and drums. Todd had a wide array of influences and loved everything from metal to punk and everything in between. Our worlds eventually clashed, and we parted ways. I don't remember being very happy about the breakup or even exactly how it all came about. It just came to an end. We were at our peak and maybe that was enough of a reason at the time. After all, "No future!" had been our battle cry for our generation of punk. I was angry and hurt, maybe because I didn't have the vision or foresight that Jack may have possessed, or maybe I just didn't want it to end. We were riding together, but we were also on different journeys. Years later, Jack told me that he never realized that I cared so much about the band and what we had.

I was lucky to still have Ron by my side. Ron's an amazing writer, my favorite guitarist, and my lifelong friend. During this time, the two of us never stopped writing. In fact, "Red Shadows" was one of the bass lines/songs slated for our next record. Ron and I rehearsed at Jerry "Potato Head" Hurtado's (RIP) house in a room in the back he used as a studio.

We were there every day, just me and Ron, writing, rewriting, and so on. We played all day most evenings, and some nights, and still managed to hit the clubs, but this time with a new agenda. We were looking for a new band or at least a vocalist and a drummer.

During this time, I don't believe Jack missed a beat and had Cathedral of Tears up and running in record time. He may have been working on it with new bandmates prior to TSOL ending. He still had Greg and Todd along with him, although Greg was playing with Bob Dylan and Cathedral of Tears simultaneously. This may have caused some turmoil with Jack, so Greg ended up leaving Cathedral altogether. During the time of the split, we would speak and even see each other once in a while. Jack amazes me to this day with his talent and the ease with which he moves through musical styles, his vision, command, and understanding of what he wants and how to achieve it. We were just in search of something different at the time.

Ron and I searched the clubs, as often as possible, looking to cherry-pick from bands we watched, hoping to steal or entice them to come along with us and join our band. We waded through endless amounts of bands playing at local clubs. I couldn't help but be overwhelmed by the size of the task at hand. We were trying to find the right pieces to our puzzle that would become our band. I think we were looking for a type of energy over talent. We didn't need "Rock Stars" we needed bandmates. It's funny how that worked out. We knew how to do it and knew what we wanted.

ELECTRIC CHAIR

I had a friend who used to sit around with me at Sunline Surfboards where we would talk about opening a punk rock store in Orange County. As luck would have it, he beat me to it and was able to open the first punk rock store, London Exchange, in Costa Mesa. They were always crushing it, bringing punk rock fashion to OC. I had the idea for Electric Chair because living in Orange County, we had to go to Hollywood to get Creepers, Doc Martin boots, and other punk attire. It took me a while to do it, but I finally convinced Abdul, my boss at Sunline, to front me a little money to open a very small shop on Main Street, in HB. The location I found was a doorway next to George's Surf Center. The spot was just a six-foot-wide hallway, twenty or so feet deep, with a high ceiling. A doorway and a window above it were the only sources of air and light. I had a budget and was very limited in what I was able to carry out. My only option was shelves on the walls, as there was no room for free standing racks. I had a 3 to 4 foot wide sales counter at one end, but basically it was just a hallway. We had three styles of creepers, t-shirts, buttons, and not much else.

The shop was enough of a success that we combined Sunline and Electric Chair and moved to a larger location on the corner of Main Street and Walnut, where the old Terry's Drug Store used to be. The front of the store was filled with surf stuff, while Electric Chair was set up in the back corner of the store. There was a step-up space where the old pharmacy prescriptions counter was, and it had the prescriptions sign hanging from the drop ceiling. We left that sign up the whole time the store was open. Surf wear items such as Quicksilver, Gotcha, Billabong, etc., along with all the surfboards and boogie boards filled out the front of the shop. It was quite a big space, and although I had my doubts in the beginning about combining punk clothing and surf wear, it worked flawlessly. Within a few years, I had expanded what I was selling to alternative clothing, shoes, boots, creepers, t-shirts, belts, hats, and some shit for the counter like, buttons, bracelets, stickers, and sunglasses. But I was still lacking really cool clothing, original shirts, posters, records, and tapes. What I wanted was "REAL" punk rock fashion. The stuff you would find at Ray and Dang's Trash and Vaudeville on Saint Marks Place in New York. At the time, you couldn't find very many punk rock clothing stores stateside, and certainly not many in Orange County. So, what to do? Go to England! It took a little convincing to get Abdul to see the benefit versus the cost, but he did, and soon I was off to England. I went solo which would be the case for many more trips to follow. I stayed in Earl's Court, made a couple connections, and tried to make more. I shopped at Camden Market and King's Road, walking or taking the tube everywhere. I bought giant suitcases and stuffed them full, with more than I could carry, and somehow, I got it all to the airport. I boarded my flight home and breezed through customs. I was back home with tons of stuff from England that nobody else had; I couldn't be happier.

In the early days of punk rock, you couldn't even buy a t-shirt with a skull and crossbones on it, let alone Creepers, Doc Martins, or Beatle boots. This was the beginning of a fashion pilgrimage that I made every few months to England. After a while, we were able to buy most of the stuff in the States. Thanks to NANA in Santa Monica for filling the void, I was able to get shoes and other items without having to travel to the UK. Electric Chair was the second punk rock store in Orange County and the longest running. I'm proud of what we accomplished during my time there.

Everything was going well; I was touring nonstop, putting out records, and Electric Chair was killing it, apart from my drug use, which was becoming more like work than fun. Once again, it was time for a tour, but we had just lost our manager at Electric Chair. Abdul was in a fuss about it, as I was leaving on tour and wasn't there to handle things. As luck would have it, Ron's girlfriend, Sara, who managed a t-shirt shop in Laguna Beach had just lost her job. Perfect; I knew her, she was Ron's girl, what could go wrong?

I began to notice during my usual calls home to my store, that I was starting to get less and less information and a colder tone. Abdul had taken quite a liking to Sara. She had put it out there that I wasn't needed anymore; after all, I was never there anyway. He still wanted me to call in on ideas, although I was told they didn't need me dropping by anymore. Dropping by? I was the creator, manager, buyer, and obviously too trusting.

Abdul had recently lost his wife, and I'm sure he enjoyed Sara's company and attention. During and after the tour, my drug use had increased exponentially. I didn't deal very well with losing control of the company I built, and I felt betrayed. In my strung-out head, I thought I was bulletproof and decided to tell Abdul to buy me out. I figured I'd be back; I did it once, I could do it again. But lightning seldom strikes in the same place twice, and I settled for way less than I deserved. Acting too much on emotion is never a good way to conduct business and being strung out is no way to conduct life. The money was probably gone in less than a month. I should've left things as they were, retaining my 10% of monthly sales. My emotions got the better of me and I agreed to a buyout, and that chapter in my life was over, just like that.

CHANGE TODAY

I don't remember who we approached first, Joe or Mitch, but we had gone to the Music Machine in West Hollywood to see The Joneses with whom Ron was the original guitar player. I remember liking how hard Mitch hit the snare drum. He played solid and basic, which is what we were looking for because we could never find a comparable drummer to replace Todd. I had tried and tried to get Todd to continue with us and I know he was torn, but he was very loyal to Jack. He went on to play with a couple of Jack's next bands, Cathedral of Tears and Tender Fury.

At this point, we needed a vocalist. We knew Joe from around Huntington Beach. He played bass in Steve Reehl's band, The Hated. Chalmer from early Vandals also played with Joe, at some point. I believe Joe's band was called The Loners. Joe was a friend and party pal of ours, so we gave him a try. Although it was very different, his style seemed to work on the new songs. He also played rhythm guitar, which added another layer that we thought we could use. We now had all the pieces to our puzzle.

The TSOL band, as we knew it, ended in mid-1983, with Jack, Todd, and Greg departing. They formed Cathedral of Tears and released their first record in 1984. The decision to keep the name, TSOL was made by us without enough thought. We rationalized that it was okay, and we knew it would allow us to keep moving at a quick pace. I even approached Jack and told him of our intention to keep the name, he laughed and said that's what he would do. Now, I think he was just talking shit or possibly drunk, as we were at a bar. He would've never kept the name; it's not his style. As for me, it was one of the biggest mistakes. I should've left the name behind; we could've stood on our own.

By January of '84, we were doing shows as the new TSOL. We began touring immediately and we must've done thirty shows before April of

'84. The *Change Today* album was released just five months after starting the band. We did over a hundred shows in '84 and had opportunities and access to clubs across the nation. I believe, initially, because we kept the name. Some fans got it, others didn't. We played hard and non-stop; we had to sell it all over again. Having a new record out helped. *Change Today* was recorded at Madd Dog Studio in Venice, CA. Chris Grayson, our soundman on this album also worked with Dead Kennedys. *Change Today* was a good effort, full of honest, powerful, and stripped-down cuts; the band was tight. All we did was play, practice, drink, and play some more.

Around the time between *Change Today* and *Revenge*, we found a high-energy manager, Mike Zoto, that saw something in us. He tried repeatedly to sign us until we finally gave in. He had big ideas and a grand plan, and I believe he did his best until the very end. I know he wanted us to be more commercial; that could have had something to do with where we finally ended up. We weren't quite as polished as the *Hit and Run* record cover made us seem. (*Thank you, Neil Zlozower, photographer to the stars.*) We were rougher around the edges; as it turned out, we were a cracked and crumbling unit. We had become a product of our environment and a sign of the times. As an artist, I believe it was up to us to set the trend and not follow it. I have to take responsibility for my part in how it ended and what we had become.

This was the time when the skateboarding scene started gathering around our cause by supporting our shows. It didn't hurt that Ron and I had always skated when we were on tour. We took our boards with us everywhere. Ron happened to be quite good and well connected with the skateboarding community in general. We got a lot of support from the skate magazine, *Thrasher*, which was founded in '81 by Eric Swenson and Fausto Vitello. Like us, many other punk bands were also skateboarders, so it went hand in hand. Thrasher released a music compilation series titled, *Skate Rock* which was a cassette as well as sold on vinyl. It featured a couple of our songs on *Volume Two* which came out during '84 when we were touring heavy for *Change Today*. Thrasher introduced a lot of new skaters to bands they may not have heard of otherwise. Every time we played San Francisco, we visited Thrasher. The guys were always great to us and seemed to be at almost every show in San Francisco.

Shows were starting to get more crowded, and we were developing a fan base. From time to time there was still some confusion with fans expecting to hear early songs which we tried not to do. The band's dynamic was working well, and in theory, we were all pretty much equals. We had a crew of Chris Grayson, our driver, sound man, and holdover from the Dead Kennedys, and Eric Arab as our catch-all-do-all roadie. We had a van and a trailer that we owned, and since we pretty much felt lost if we weren't working, we stayed on tour as much as possible. I think we all enjoyed the gypsy lifestyle, town to town, different clubs, different girls, different bars, and so on. It's funny that at that time in Texas, it was legal to drink and drive, but you would go to jail for having a joint.

Drugs, at this point, were still more of a pastime rather than an occupation for me. Weed helped make the long hours and long drives somewhat bearable. Drinking was mandatory, as we were all heavy drinkers and beer was affordable, as most of the clubs had beer on tap, and sometimes it was free. We liked our whiskey too and fancied ourselves as hard drinkers; after all, we had been practicing for years. On tour, coke was a luxury for us because it was so expensive, but at home, it was everywhere. I don't remember how much we messed with speed, but for long drives, I'm sure it was helpful at times. Joe and I dabbled in heroin when it was available, and in cities like New York, it was on every corner. Ron occasionally messed with heroin, smoked, and drank like the rest of us; Mitch liked coke and beer. Joe would give you his last dollar if he could, but we weren't making much money, so I usually bought the drugs. We called Joe "Joey Oweie," at the time. I still had an income stream coming in from Electric Chair, my punk rock clothing store.

The band toured as much as possible for over a year. You could only play so much at home, so we traveled coast to coast and everywhere in between. We enjoyed it, although it wasn't glamorous. It was a lot of hard work, but as a young man, that's all I wanted to do. By mid '86, we were in the studio again recording the *Revenge* album. *Revenge* was recorded at the Music Grinder Studios in Hollywood on Enigma Records and produced by Howard Benson. The sound was a bit of a departure from *Change Today* and reflected our growth as a band. To this day, I still hate the sound of the snare on that record. In my opinion, it was unnecessarily processed.

We had a couple of solid tracks off *Revenge*; Nothing for You was featured in the 1985 movie, *The Return of the Living Dead*. It was also our first video. The song, "Revenge" was also featured in a movie called, *Dangerously Close* in 1986. We made a video for our song, "Colors" off the same album. I'm not sure of the total sales of *Revenge*, but the album was a success in my eyes.

After the release of *Revenge*, we secured the opening spot on the Red Hot Chili Peppers American tour that took us to; Austin, St. Louis, Kansas, Minneapolis, Toronto, Ottawa, Richmond, DC, and NY, just to name a few of the stops. The tour lasted a month and ended in LA. Each band had a van and a trailer. The Peppers had their manager, Lindy Goetz, and Mr. Mark "Do-it-all" Johnson, who not only drove, but was their roadie, unloaded van, and carried their luggage from room to van, etc. He did it all. The crowd's reaction to the Peppers during the tour was electric, and we just knew this was going to be big.

We had "Arab," Eric Groff, our go-to guy, our ride-or-die friend who still works with us till this day. We also had our manager at the time, Mike Zoto, and sound man, Chris Grayson with us. When we were on our way to the Canadian border, our managers had told all of us to get rid of everything, any sign or trace of paraphernalia. So, in our van, we did this by tossing it out of the back window and I assumed the following van did as well. Joe ended up still having some shit left in his suitcase, but luckily the border agents didn't find it. Honestly, we toured so much during that time, that the shows all tend to blur together in my mind. The bill pushed us every night and we played well. It was fun and the Chili Peppers were on fire. I often spent my time after shows eating and having coffee with Hillel (RIP), when possible. We finished that tour on January 9, 1987.

For the bass players out there; to my knowledge, Flea had never used GK gear before that tour. We combined our two SVT 8/10 cabinets for max bass, and when I showed him my head, he didn't know what it was but seemed to like it after using it. The interesting part is that today, Flea is one of GK's top endorsers and has been for many years.

Hit and Run followed in July '87 on Enigma/Capitol records. Howard Benson was the producer once again. This became our only release to chart the Billboard 200, reaching number 184. I couldn't see it coming at the time but *Hit and Run* was the beginning of the end for Ron, who would leave after the recording. After that, I was the only original member remaining. I believe it had all just become too much for him, with the image, management, drug addictions, egos, etc. I think Ron wanted out of the train wreck that we had become." I also think Ron wanted to be normal, or more normal. Ron stuck around for the filming of the video for the Name is Love but was soon gone. This left me with a bit of a problem, firstly Ron was my best friend and secondly, Ron and I had created a true democracy. I was now easily and often outvoted; it was two against one.

In 1988 we landed the opening spot on the Guns N Roses tour. This was a big deal since they chose us over Faster Pussy Cat and Junkyard who were bands on major labels. It didn't hurt our notoriety when GNR drummer Steven Adler wore a TSOL t-shirt in the "Sweet Child O' Mine" music video. Years ago, I mentioned in an interview that I hear more people telling me about seeing our t-shirt in that video more than anything we've ever done. On the last night of that tour, in Phoenix, Axl decided not to show up. Near the end of our set, we were signaled to keep playing. We were left to jam cover songs until finally it was announced that GNR had canceled.

Following Ron's departure, we had a couple guitarists who tried out while we were looking for a replacement. Scotty Phillips and Mike Eldred were both gifted guitar players. Mike played a show with us at the Coach House one night and absolutely killed it. Although we ended up going with Scotty because he "fit the image." To this day, I believe Mike would have been the perfect choice. Mike went on to run the Fender custom shop for years and remained a close friend. Enter Marshall Rohner, a truly gifted guitar player who we all knew. He had played with the Cruzados,

Jimmy and the Mustangs, and a few others. The problem was, he brought many issues of his own, one of which was he had been a heroin addict for years.

It's not to say that we weren't good; we were tight, and the record had some strong songs, "Sixteen," "Hit and Run," and "The Name is Love." "Sixteen" was my favorite song to play live off that record, although "The Name is Love" was the video.

Playing live was what we were all about, and everything else we had to go through seemed tolerable when we were playing. But external and internal pressures and our distorted perception, I think, had allowed us to drift away from our ultimate goals with which we had started. We had become a product in a package, ready to be sold. The fact that I was totally strung out didn't help either. Joe was strung out as well, and Mitch was a total cokehead and hard drinker. We all drank heavily, in fact, they both admitted to having problems with drugs and alcohol and claimed to have cleaned up after I was fired.

Strange Love was released in 1990 on Enigma/Capitol. We had 30 songs written for Strange Love and had worked with Jim Faraci at the world-famous Village recording studios, in West LA. The Village was housed in a 1920s Masonic temple. Jim worked there and got us in on spec time which is basically free until your record deal comes through and you get some money, then it's assumed you begin paying for the studio time. We never went back to record there because our manager, Mike, was trying to sell us on some producer, John Janson who had some recent success with a couple of hard rock acts and a lofty resume. I was familiar with him, or at least a couple of his records. The rest of the band, along with our manager, were interested, so Mike gave him our demos that Jim Faraci had recorded and produced. I wasn't too happy with this; I liked the demos we did at The Village and was happy with the direction in which we were going. I also felt a deal was a deal and we had agreed to work with Jim. So, when we met John Janson at our lock-out rehearsal studio, I was less than enthused, but listened to him anyway.

What unfolded in that meeting, to this day, still amazes me. The producer, John, said he had listened to the demos, and here was his plan;

he wanted to use the intro of song one, with the chorus from song number two, the break of song number twelve, etc. Basically, he was cutting and pasting together our songs by mixing and matching parts from existing songs and creating new versions to his liking. To my surprise and disgust, my bandmates, Joe, Mitch, and manager, Mike were nodding their heads in agreement. Marshall wasn't there, but that was another story. Song after song, he detailed his new arrangement for each song and his choice of lyrics. I really couldn't believe the ease with which they gave up our vision for each song. After all the hard work writing those songs, somehow it was okay with them to go with this crazy ass piecemeal method of rearranging each one, and to top it off, they agreed to pay him $30,000!

I believe we missed the mark horribly with the *Strange Love* release.

Strange Love was recorded at Sunset Sound Factory and Crystal Sound in Los Angeles in September 1989; it was our last studio album. The truth is, they kicked me out. They carried on for a few more years touring without me, but *Strange Love* was a big disappointment to fans and critics. The album was way overproduced, in my opinion, and Enigma eventually dropped them.

Not that it mattered much for me, as I was fired one day into a club tour. We had started on the West Coast after we finished recording. As it happened, we played a little club in the Bay Area. After the show Marshall disappeared, and was gone for hours, and as Joe, Mitch, and I sat there waiting and wondering what happened to Marshall, (*he went to buy some dope and get high*) we started arguing. I was kicking dope again. I had some meds but was far from well. This was just part of the deal if you were an addict, and I had prepared to detox again. But this time around Joe and Mitch were blaming me for Marshall taking off saying, we were both dope fiends, fuck ups, etc. The funny thing was, I had no part in Marshall being gone, and neither Joe, Mitch, nor myself were clean at this point. The later it got, the more heated the argument grew, with me being singled out as the problem. I finally got up from where I was trying to sleep in the van and accosted Mitch. I grabbed him by the collar and said, "Yes I'm a dope fiend, but you're a fucking dirtbag so,

Fuck Off!" I was sick of his shit! On more than one occasion, his indiscretions put me in uncomfortable situations. He knew exactly what I meant, and to save his reputation, pinned his bad behavior on me.

Joe hailed a cab, and then he and Mitch walked around the front of the van, got in, and left. They were gone, off to the airport to fly home, the tour was over, leaving me with the van, trailer, and equipment, and still waiting for Marshall. Marshall finally showed up, (RIP), fucking idiot. We were done after only one show into the tour. To cover their tracks, Joe and Mitch called Mike, our manager, and made arrangements to get off drugs…detox…or so the story went.

I was out of TSOL, fired from my own band by a manager and members I hired. I think they had the idea that the record would be a big hit. It wasn't, and in my opinion, it was our worst. I wasn't happy about being fired but in all fairness, there wasn't much left of the band that I loved. I was lost, we were lost and had been adrift for a while. Heroin and drugs in general surely didn't help, but it would still be years before I was able to figure that out or to get clean. I used this as an excuse to go deeper into my addiction; self-pity is a motherfucker. An addict making business decisions was, in my case, not a very good idea.

Mike Zoto, Joe, and Mitch wanted to control and own the TSOL name outright. I dealt with Mike Zoto on this and really don't remember whose idea it was, or rather who approached who first. Feeling as if I had already lost everything, I felt that it was a way to get something back from all my years of work. We settled on a number and agreed they would make monthly installments until I was paid in full. I had no idea what a bad decision this was at the time because I felt I had nothing to lose. It took me years to realize the enormity of this mistake, effectively losing all control of the band and its name, but I felt I had no choice. With the deal with the Devil now done, they started to make their payments. The payments lasted for a while, but I guess business wasn't so good because soon after we made the deal, they just stopped. I called Zoto and asked, what's up, and he said, "We're done paying." They still owed a substantial amount to me, so I went to a local club, Joshuas Marquee Club in Garden Grove, where they were playing one night to confront them.

When I walked in, they looked like they had seen a ghost. Mitch saw me, turned, and walked or rather quickly scurried in the other direction. Dave, their new bass player was wrapping a timing chain belt around his fist, as if they were going to fight me. All of this seemed silly to me. I approached Joe and asked, "What's up, why aren't you guys paying?" He said they were done paying. I told him what he already knew; that they still owed at least four to six grand. During this time, the original TSOL lineup had a standing offer to do reunion shows. I told Joe, "If you guys don't pay the money you agreed to, I'm going to do the reunion shows." His response was, "We're not going to pay you, so do what you gotta do." It seemed that they didn't think the original band reforming, even just for a show, would affect them. In my humble opinion, it did. It actually buried them.

Years later, and only with considerable talent, effort, and sheer balls did Jack eventually right the ship and restore the name to its rightful owners. (I'm Not Always Right) — M.R.

THE REUNION

In December 1989 there had been an offer on the table, for a while, from Gary and Paul at Goldenvoice to do a reunion show. The old members of TSOL and I hadn't been communicating at the time, and I believed doing a reunion show would be counterproductive. Furthermore, I believed Jack and the guys had no desire or plans to continue after a one-off show. This made me question the value beyond making a little money, and it was quite possible that one show could hinder or bury the progress made with the new TSOL. I was the last member to come on board for the reunion show. With me as the sole holdout, or rather the last one to give consent, it only took a simple yes from me to get the ball rolling. The show was to be at the Celebrity Theater in the Round, with the audience on all sides, the stage being circular, and could be rotated while you were playing. The opening bands were to be: The Offspring and Cadillac Tramps as direct support with us headlining. The Offspring were a new band and big TSOL fans.

The problem was, we weren't a band anymore. Jack was playing and recording with his band, Tender Fury; Ron was working and playing in his new band, Lunch Box, and I was completely strung out and floundering. I was pawning everything I owned and anything else I could get my hands on, usually borrowed equipment. I asked Jack how much we were getting paid for the show, and he said he had already been paid, in fact, everyone had already been paid. What? So, I made up some number in my head, went to Gary, and told him that's what I wanted. Gary came back and said, "Awww come on, Mike, that's too much." After a bit of wrangling, we settled on a price for my involvement. I arranged to collect weekly, oftentimes daily, trying to stay well up until the show. But as it got closer to show time, I had spent all the money in the weeks and days before we even played. I continued to pawn every bass that I borrowed, begged, or stole on my road to ruin.

I had no idea who The Offspring were, how big of fans of TSOL they were, or how huge they would become. Nor did I realize how great of a band the Cadillac Tramps were. I was in a dope-fueled haze, well into a heavy downward spiral. I was depressed, strung out, and addicted. I had always drunk booze, smoked weed, and sniffed coke and speed, but I had let heroin pretty much take over my life at this point. I don't ever really remember calling it heroin, it was always balloons, black tar, or chiva. I never thought of myself as an addict, it was just normal drinking, smoking, snorting coke, etc. Youth was a party with few consequences, you're bulletproof right up until you're bullet-ridden. The day of the show was hectic; once again I had no equipment, a borrowed bass, and no amps. Luckily Chris Grayson, our sound man, had just arrived home from a Red Hot Chili Peppers tour with all of Flea's new Mesa Boogie gear in the truck. Problem solved; in came this massive amount of high-tech bass gear. Not mine, I had never used it before, but I did own a Boogie head at some point. It still was not the same. Although Chris tried to make it sound good, it was too punchy and too loud on stage and probably had a few too many cabinets. The show was a blur. I came out wearing a skull mask. Jack said I looked the same with it off or on… Fuck. Todd was tweaking out of his mind, and I was loaded; Ron and Jack had to have been mortified. We got through the set, and at that point, Jack and Ron were happy to put some distance between us. Neither Todd nor I were anywhere near ready to clean up yet. It seems to me, looking back, that the closer you were to me, the worse it was for you. I was on a path of self-destruction and there was no end in sight.

We played a few more shows over the next year or so. We were billed under the names LOST and Superficial Love for legal reasons, as Joe and Mitch still owned the TSOL name. I laid it out there and did exactly what I said, we buried them. We played the first reunion show before *Strange Love* was even released. We weren't really an active band at this point, but we came together as a band for these events. We were all coming together for a payday that we rightfully deserved.

On 2/1/1991 we played as LOST at the Hollywood Palladium with Bad Religion. Then on 3/23/91 we played at UCI Crawford Hall, billed as Superficial Love. Todd and I were still totally fucked up.

During this time, I had a girlfriend, Claudia, who felt compelled to be with me even though most of my desirable traits had disappeared. She was an addict with underlying health issues which she ignored despite several warning signs. We moved around quite a bit and the main focus for us, at the time, was staying high. We were selling drugs, whenever possible, to make ends meet. Most of our time was spent in Long Beach, which was a little friendlier than Huntington Beach, meaning our behavior seemed to go a bit more unnoticed, as Long Beach still had more of an inner-city vibe. HB had that behind the Orange Curtain feel, beachy, with a small-town mentality. I was hassled less and closer to my connections in Long Beach. I had a large group of friends, and we all had the same problems. Even so, it soon became more comfortable for us to move to Hollywood, as it was becoming too hot, harder to fly under the radar even in Long Beach. First, we lived with Scotty, one of the later guitarists in TSOL, and his girlfriend in West Hollywood. Then we moved into a house with a guy called Worm from HB. A couple I knew from the Hollywood punk scene, Iris Berry, a musician at that time and now a writer and publisher, and Mad Marc Rude, a Hollywood tattooist and artist (RIP) had just moved out. So, my girlfriend, my dog, and I moved into one of the rooms of the three-bedroom house close to Hollywood Forever cemetery. I was making a living by dealing heroin and speed. I'd buy in Long Beach and sell in LA for more money to my clientele of rockers, punks, and general deviants with the same bad habits as myself. I always liked Hollywood and it was nice to be away from Long Beach despite my weekly, sometimes daily, drives back for drugs. In Los Angeles, you usually had to go downtown and buy off the street which was dangerous on many levels. For my clientele, it was more comfortable for some to buy from me rather than a stranger.

Being that I lived in a working-class neighborhood, there weren't many fancy cars on my street. Some of my clients were rockstars which I had become friends with over the years, mostly because we had the same interest, whether it was music or drugs, we just got along. I would generally arrange to meet them at a location or sometimes at my house, whatever was most convenient and safe. Oftentimes, they were in as much of a hurry as I was to get them their heroin. I was also in a hurry to get the fuck out of Long Beach, away from Metro police, and back home, hopefully avoiding attention in the Highway Patrol-infested territory I drove through.

To my shock and dismay, often I would come home to find a really nice car in front of my house clearly waiting for me. One day, I came home to a Corvette, Jaguar, and Mercedes Benz parked directly in front of my house. I walked in-yelling, "You can't fucking park these cars in front of my house. Are you kidding me?" All nice guys, all my friends, and all with the same bad habits as me, at the time. I would try to stagger them as they left the house in hopes of drawing less attention to my business, if that was even possible, just another day in the hood.

Life was going along as normally as it could be living in a house full of junkies in the middle of Hollywood. We would all talk about wishing we were normal, with a regular life, a regular job, and regular problems, I certainly did. Worm had a job, his girlfriend didn't work, I hustled, and my girlfriend didn't work either. There was another roommate, but I don't remember who. Worm and I talked of quitting many times. My girlfriend, Claudia, was frail to start with, and the constant use of drugs wasn't doing her any favors. She had partied and used speed for years, and even though I knew better, I let her do dope as if I could stop her. One day she was feeling under the weather, so we went to the doctor, and he said she really needed to stop; she had an issue with her heart. I left the doctor's office with a new resolve and went home to speak to Worm. He agreed, or so he said, that we all needed to stop.

We made plans to quit right away. I was done and we were all going to kick. Much easier said than done, but I felt we had to, she had to.

The next few days were rough, really rough; we had all been on a very long run and we were sick, the kind of sick you only know if you've kicked heroin and speed at the same time. Zero sleep, cramps all over your body, horrible cramps in your legs, throwing up, and everything hurts. I think, in theory, the kicking speed part should have helped overall because you might just want to sleep, but the heroin won't let you; it just wants to punish you for leaving. It's horrible and cruel; there's nothing quite like it, and I've heard many an addict say they don't have another kick in them. I believe it's true; get out while you can and stay out. Heroin is a cruel joke and a terrible lie. We sweated and cried, rolled around on the bed, and suffered. After a few days, we felt a tiny bit better, enough to get up and get some soda and some food, so we walked to the local neighborhood market with our dog, Elvis. When we got home, dead tired and sweaty from a short walk, I noticed we had guests, or rather Worm had three guests. As we walked in, Worm went to his room and locked the door. This should've been a sign to me, but at that point, it was too late anyway. I knew one of the guys, his name was Dana, he was an old HB punk, a bit younger than me. He didn't look like the punk I remembered, but it had been many years.

One of the last times I saw Dana, we had tracked him down after he robbed our studio at Todd's house and stole Ron's Les Paul, which we recovered. Soon after the guitar incident, I went to Borzoo's house where he and his buddy John were beating Dana in the kitchen. They stopped when I arrived, and I tried to defuse the situation. John and Borzoo were planning on taking Dana to the desert and shooting him. He was their friend by the way. It seems they had just bought matching rifles and wanted to try them out. Really!!! That's what they said, and I did my best to squash this shit and calm everybody down. I put Dana in my car and took him home. I'm sure I saw him over the years, but it had been a while.

Dana, it seemed, didn't recognize me that day he came into my house. One of the other guys, who I later learned his name was Zippy, had a gun and we were now being corralled into the living room at gunpoint. Zippy told me that if my dog acted up or we tried anything he would shoot my dog. I said, "Please don't shoot my dog." He kept suggesting that I go to my room and get my guns. I didn't have a gun and told him, "I don't have a gun." This went on for a while as they taunted us pointing the gun at my girl, me, and my dog. All the while Worm stayed in his room. It seems our plan to quit didn't work for them because they were Worm's drug dealers and they didn't want him to quit. He must have told them I was the problem, and so we had to go. I was roughed up a little bit and showed the door. I was thankful we weren't hurt and he didn't shoot my dog. I later learned the quiet one was the leader, Ron; actually they were all sober gangsters.

We were on the street in Hollywood with a few possessions and our dog, Elvis. I figured I would deal with Worm, Dana, and Zippy later. As it turned out, the only one I ever had any dealings with again was Ron. Zippy was later run out of OC under a cloud of suspicion that he molested a roommate's daughter. I guess karma is a mother fucker because I was now paying for some of my bad behavior, the only problem was my girlfriend and Elvis were too. When you have nobody else you can call or turn to, who do you call? I called my mom.

We were now back in OC, Westminster to be exact. My mom and her husband were gracious enough to take us in; we were barely clean, less than a week with our dog, Elvis in tow. They were lifesavers; we had nowhere else to go. My mom set about trying to get us healthy, feeding us, and helping in any way she could. John, her husband, was super tolerant, never complained or made us feel uncomfortable. I would take long walks with my dog to a large park near the house and it seemed to help being active. My girlfriend, on the other hand, wasn't bouncing back as fast. She never wanted to get out of bed, complained, and always wanted to argue with me. She wasn't happy being clean and didn't want anything to do with recovery meetings. She was shy at times anyway, but this was beyond that, I just couldn't get her involved or motivated.

I was contacted by an old friend and asked if I wanted to join their band. I met them and listened to their demo and liked the elements. The vocals reminded me of Steve Marriott and the guitarist was a monster. I told them I didn't want to join their band, but I would be interested in forming a new one, and a new project was born. So, at first, we started rehearsing in some studios between the Valley and OC. I still had some equipment in pawn and eventually was able to get my Thunderbird bass back. We were writing and reworking some songs practicing five nights a week. My girlfriend wasn't interested and caused giant fights almost every night when I got home, which was causing a bit of a strain on our guest status at my mom's. Screaming, yelling, and breaking things in the room was common. I just couldn't get her out of bed; she was miserable all the time. She wasn't bouncing back very quickly, if at all, and I couldn't get her to do anything. I truly loved her, but our relationship was becoming strained. She didn't like me going out, but she didn't want to go with me and if I went anyway, World War III erupted every time I got home. We were growing apart, but we were never completely able to let go for years to come. I was getting better and she was not.

The band was coming along. It was nice having a purpose again.

It was something I knew how to do and it kept me pushing forward. Next song, next rehearsal, recording, and eventually even a show. It was, at least, something positive and productive. I was starting to feel alive again. It had been a while since I felt human and I started going to see bands here and there, trying to gauge where we might fit in.

I moved into a cabana behind my guitarist's house in the Valley, as my girlfriend and I had separated. I was pretty broke, cash-poor as they say; every once in awhile a royalty check would appear out of nowhere, usually just in the nick of time. I began to move on and was starting to see a new girl, Kristen who years later would become my first wife. The breakup with Claudia was anything but clean, it was messy, ugly, and hard. Little did I know the tangled web of drugs and dysfunction would haunt me and the ones I cared about in one way or another for years to come.

We called the band Big American Dogs. We played a couple shows, recorded a demo, and hammered away just like everyone else. It was definitely a rock band, but we never gained much traction or got very far. I don't think it helped that I had rediscovered speed… I mean, I thought it totally helped, but of course, it didn't. Speed is three steps forward four steps back. I was of the naive opinion that speed was never a problem like heroin was, so what could go wrong? Plus, I was able to work and play harder, and longer, drink more, and still get shit done. Oh ya, I also thought it was still okay to drink. I just didn't get it and still wouldn't for a while, a long while. But, at that moment, things were still okay, or so I thought.

Life was just a party again, playing, practicing, and hanging out with my girlfriend whenever possible. Yeah, I hurt my first girlfriend moving on, but things were not good. We were fighting, having dog custody issues, and it was turning out to be a messy breakup with her doing drive-bys of my place, etc. Oh yeah, and I was slipping back into a bad place of thinking I could manage this because, at least I wasn't using heroin. Famous last words.

I continued a slow slide back into my old behavior. A bumpy path leading down to that dark place, void of any light or sanity that might have otherwise saved me and others from myself. Really what all this means is, that I was using drugs again more frequently, if not regularly. I started chipping again, meaning using little bits of heroin. I don't remember how much or how little or if my girlfriend was using heroin at all. It wouldn't have mattered anyway because eventually everybody was strung out. There was a new kind of user, the big lie that was "heroin chic." It seemed everybody in my circle was using heroin and speed. Heroin seemed to insulate me from my world of chaos. Speed kept the edge where I could hustle enough to keep up the frantic pace and constant consumption. This went on for a while and the time with my new band was coming to an end.

I had been staying with my new girlfriend, Kristen, in Santa Monica from time to time while living in the cabana behind Mark, my bandmate's house. Mark had decided he wanted to move into the cabana so he could rent the front house out to Robbin Crosby (RIP). Robin had stayed with us in the Santa Monica apartment, occasionally. He was a sweetheart, a gentle giant, if you will, but the worst kind of drug addict, roommate one could imagine, helpless, needy, and at times a danger to himself and others. When Robbin moved out of our apartment and into Mark's house, we had a falling out over some equipment, drugs, money, or all three. Robin and I were friends and even went to Cabo together to try and kick drugs, at one point. To this day, with twenty-plus years of sobriety, this is one of my greatest regrets, that I never got to see him to make amends before he passed.

Kristen and I were spending more and more time in Long Beach in our pursuit of drugs and hanging out with like-minded friends. One day would turn into three days as we bounced around, couch surfing with no real responsibility in the way of work. Our days were spent in search of getting and using drugs. As bad as this was, we believed we were just partying and had it under control. I think most of the time we tried not to think at all. It may have seemed to us that it was a slow downward slide, but to anyone on the outside and especially to her family, it looked more like we were jumping off a cliff.

I was pretty bad; I meant well, but my actions seldom matched up with my true self or rather my old self. It was like driving down a foggy road, so foggy you couldn't see the line dividing the lanes, so you constantly drift from your lane into the oncoming traffic of the other lane and back again. In my case, it was from right to wrong, and back again. My behavior was taking a toll on me, Kristen, and our relationship. It was also driving me to be more and more down on myself; I felt I didn't deserve any better. My guilt and remorse made me feel like I didn't deserve anything at all.

HIGH DESERT

In 1992, I received a message from my sister that my father had committed suicide. I don't remember how she reached me, as I was couch hopping at that time, flopping around, and certainly didn't have a phone. As soon as I got the news, I called my mom, and she confirmed he had shot himself and it had something to do with the police. As distant as we had become and had been for many years, this hit me hard in a strange kind of way. My father's brother, David, committed suicide when I was four years old.

My mom, her husband, John, Coleen, and her husband, Greg were all headed to Apple Valley in the high desert where my father lived. I didn't make it until the next day, but when I arrived, they were all in the garage talking. My dad's Filipino mail-ordered bride, Grace, had been there the day before crying about how George, my dad, had all the money and she had nothing. My mom had found six thousand dollars in a toolbox drawer and gave it to Grace to help her in her dilemma. As it turns out, Grace had called the police on my dad for growing marijuana, even though she lived there and watered the plants. I had proof of this when I found letters with how much her family owed my dad and a calendar with the watering schedule in her handwriting. My dad had these stashed above the water heater in the garage, as he was seemingly going to divorce her and was keeping track of what he would owe to her and what was owed to him.

The incident unfolded when the police arrived and questioned him about growing marijuana. He admitted it but didn't have the experience or knowledge of how to handle the situation. He never did drugs and barely drank. I'm sure a friend of his taught him how to grow weed as an income; due to his age, he was no longer working like he used to. Had he known at the time to tell the cops to fuck off and come back with a warrant, everything would've unfolded differently, in my opinion. What happened instead was the cops were outside the fenced yard, my dad and his dog were inside, and they asked him if he was growing weed. While standing inside the front door he said, "Yes." They asked him if it was a lot, he said, "Yes." They told him to chain up his dog and come outside. He shut the door, walked into his bedroom, and shot himself. The cops heard the shot, proceeded to shoot the dog, then entered the house. Grace was not home when this all happened but arrived in time for the police to give her what money my dad had in his pocket. She gathered her jewelry and dishes and left claiming she was, "Scared of the spirit of George."

Because the house was now unattended, and this information was in the newspaper the next day for everyone to see, I had asked my mom and John if I could stay in the house, but because of my track record at the time, they refused. The house was off the beaten track and not everybody who lived around there were the kind of people you'd want to invite over. Unattended, the house started getting robbed. After the first robbery, my mom, my sister, John, and Greg returned to the home to try to repair the garage door. This was like putting a band-aid on an amputation. Nobody was staying there, and nobody was looking out for it, so the house continued to get robbed. Once I heard of the second and third robberies, I got a gun and went back to the high desert. Almost everything that could be carried out was gone. A Snap-On toolbox, hand tools, machinery, racing car motors on stands, motorcycle motors on stands, race bikes, multiple sets of leathers, boots, and three to five complete motorcycles all gone, with the garage door hanging loosely from the house. I had brought a friend with me and we proceeded to fix the garage door and chain it to the house. Being that I was still strung out, every once in a while, I had to leave and go back to the city which turned out to be a horrible mistake.

The house would get robbed again if I was gone for more than a day or two. Locals started to come by and ask questions and I was sure they were digging for information on how much I knew about the robberies. I later came to find out that quite a few of them were most likely involved. At this point almost everything had been stolen, certainly anything you could carry or roll away. Being that this was our inheritance and very personal to me because they were my father's possessions, I took it upon myself to get back whatever I could. I had the perfect bait for the high desert, methamphetamine.

Now, I was staying at the house and began meeting some concerned locals that were professing a great interest in helping me recover my dad's stolen property. As I said, I was rightfully suspicious of them and was convinced that some of them may have had something to do with the robberies. After all, keep your friends close and enemies closer. I started to get invited over to their homes for drinks or dinner or to share drugs. Almost everybody I met out there did meth. Occasionally, someone would bring a tool or a small piece of equipment to me saying that they found it or that they knew a guy that knew a guy. I kept notes with names and locations, and over time, started to get some idea of who was involved. I even created a board in the living room with a kind of robbery family tree with names and their suspected involvement. All the while going back to Long Beach to recharge, re-up, and eventually re-arm. By now I was carrying a gun everywhere I went. I realized that was dangerous, but so was running around the desert looking for thieves. I wanted one and all to know I was strapped 24/7 and possibly a little bit crazy. This helped keep me alive, I believe, because they do say if all the bodies in the desert stood up it would be a forest. I really wasn't a tough guy just angry, hurt, and driven.

I spoke with the detective who was in charge of my dad's suicide case and the robberies, and I found him less than helpful. At one point I asked for my dad's gun back and was told the officer who had it was on vacation. When I asked why he still had the gun, they said they didn't know, and they never did return it. Standard shit I came to find out. When they figured out a truck with a flat found near my dad's had a large piece of equipment in the back that was stolen from our house, the driver was later arrested and released. When I asked why, they said he was having a hard time and his son had attempted suicide. I mentioned my dad had committed suicide recently. They still wanted to go easy on this guy. Are YOU FUCKING KIDDING ME??? Grand theft from a home, amazing! Patrol officers did recover a stolen motorcycle that was used in a robbery, but I felt I was doing most of the work. The detectives were too busy or didn't care. Sadly, one of the biggest losses was my dad's El Camino. The car my dad had ordered from GM, custom colored black on black, it was his pride and joy since 1969. I remember my little sister and I riding in that car with the little space in the back seat going to drive-in movies.

When I had arrived early one day at my dad's house, the car had been completely stripped. The tailgate, fenders, and hood were all gone. Throughout my months there, I was able to reassemble most of the car apart from the engine and wheels. I had the car in the garage on blocks and when I returned from one of my absences, the entire car was gone once again. I searched the desert for that car, as best I could, through dirt and gravel roads, houses in the sticks, anywhere I thought it might be. I eventually found the car in a field next to a house, but everything was stripped; it was just a shell. My friend and I parked my truck, grabbed our dogs and guns, and approached the car and then the house. In a shed next to the house there was a motorcycle. It was halfway taken apart but had outlaw stickers on it. There was a large dog in a pen going crazy because he could sense us and our dogs. Suddenly out of the desert comes a pickup truck at a high rate of speed, pulling directly up to the house in a storm of dust. A woman got out of the car and approached us and asked, "What are you doing here? What do you want?" I told her, "That's my El Camino, how did it get here?" She said her husband was cooking a batch and can't be back here until tomorrow would we come back then? Being that I had identified this as an outlaw biker's house, I was a little worried about coming back the next day at an arranged time, but I agreed.

The next day, we returned to the house which I thought could possibly be fatal. I had to see this through, and I was always taught to respect, yet fear, outlaw bike clubs. We parked the car and approached the front door, each of us strapped with a concealed handgun. The disheveled lady from the day before met us looking calm, attractive, and well rested. She invited us in as she swung open the screen door and we walked in from the porch. At that very moment, I was at the height of my anxiety! What was I walking into? As I walked into the living room, there was a dark-haired man in his mid to late thirties sitting comfortably in a recliner. He immediately stood up and graciously welcomed us into his living room.

He asked if we wanted something to drink and told his wife to bring us beverages. We got straight to the El Camino with him. He apologized and told me who had sold him the car, professing he had no idea it was stolen. He was going to use the parts to restore his El Camino. He named the guy who sold it to him and I knew the name. He was a dirtbag, high desert thief like many others. He continued to apologize profusely as he did not know the origin of the car. He wanted to come to terms and pay us something. During the meeting, his wife brought out some meth and we did a line and talked more. He was friendly and seemingly honest and being a sergeant of arms of an outlaw bike club, things could've ended in a much worse way for me. I found him gracious and forthcoming. I had to come to terms that the El Camino was finally gone. Putting this behind me, I came to the realization that all the king's horses and all the king's men couldn't put the El Camino together again.

By now I had been recruiting old friends and a few new ones to come out to the desert and help me hunt. We had night vision and a few other things to help, but the longer we took, the more stuff was gone, really gone. I was making a lot of noise and causing a lot of trouble for a few guys in the high desert. I was also making a few alliances. I was lucky I didn't get shot.

I traced most of the stuff to a guy we will call "Gary." I met him and pleaded my case to him. He danced around the truth, but his name had come up many times and he didn't want the attention. He was a street racer and dealt in stolen car parts, I was told. I found some interesting stuff at his house, to say the least. I asked him to let me have a look around his yard, more of a dump really, and he finally said, "Fine, I will go with you." That was better than nothing, so we walked around his yard which was packed with odds and ends like a motor-driven cemetery. I was looking for clues and found a couple of parts boxes from my dad's house, but they were empty. Suddenly, a sheriff or local cop looked into the backyard. FUCK!!! I was carrying a loaded gun. While Gary turned to go inside and speak with the officer, I ripped my gun loose from the holster and tossed it into a bucket before he looked up at me again. Such a close call. It seems my friend sitting in his truck outside waiting for me had attracted the attention of a neighbor. In front of the cop, Gary and I pretended to be friends until he left. Like many others, Gary pretended to be sympathetic. It was hard to believe much of what he said after finding a new Chevy 388 stroker race motor on an engine stand in his garage with "ROCHE" stamped on the block. To say things were tense would be an understatement.

That was the biggest piece I had found since the police recovered the lathe (a large machinist piece of equipment generally used for making motor parts.) I pretty much focused on him after finding the race motor in his garage. Clearly, he was caught yet dismissive, telling me to get that thing out of here, as if I wasn't taking it anyway. We had also found a drag bike at another location in the Valley, with a custom-built frame, built by my father to accommodate his back injuries. I also recovered miscellaneous equipment and car and motorcycle parts that were spread across the greater area. However, I only took parts that I had paperwork on, receipts or owner's manuals, serial numbers, or documentation of some kind. At best, what I was recovering was a small fraction of that which was stolen.

Gary had moved after my first visit, but I was told where he had gone. One night, I brought a couple of friends and Elvis, on a trek to Gary's new house. This would be my last visit with him. After announcing our presence and intention and a few choice words, we entered his locked garage behind his house. What we found inside were a couple new model Mustangs, cut into pieces; we had found a chop shop! Great, that's all I needed to be involved with. In the main garage, besides multiple newish engines on stands, was an amazing amount of roll-away toolboxes, the kind master mechanics own; there must have been ten in his garage! We were working from a list, serial numbers, etc., as I said, my father had kept every receipt and owner's manual for everything he owned. We could have robbed him blind, and he deserved nothing less, but we didn't. I had two trucks and a crew with me, but we only took stuff that had belonged to my dad. One particular piece was a wood machinist box on his workbench. I knew it well, as I had seen it on a daily basis as a child; it was always sitting in the middle of my dad's workbench. When I asked

Gary about it, he told me not to touch it, that it wasn't mine. That meant nothing to me; I laughed as he was in no position to tell me anything. When I lifted the lid there was a Kawasaki Green Team sticker stuck to the inside of the box, game over. It was undoubtedly my father's, as I had known the moment that I saw it.

We ended up with my dad's Snap On rollaway but with only a few of the expensive tools that were housed in it before its theft. That roll away and its contents, like most of everything else, had been spread to the desert winds; along with race bikes, leathers, helmets, welding equipment, a lathe, mill, race motors, cars, Morris mags, a ton of specialized hand tools, the best of everything. My father's lifetime accumulation, his life's work all gone, just like that. It was gone just as quickly as he was.

The police were never much help. I had tried countless times to work with the local authorities, but they were either too busy, uninterested, or shielding some of the locals that they knew were involved. I have no idea if they knew of Gary and wanted to potentially get him on a larger charge someday or had no interest at all. Maybe they were just too busy. I doubt this type of theft was anything new to the area. It also could've been that I was an outlaw searching for justice, and they didn't appreciate my vigilante antics, or if they were even aware. I certainly looked like an outlaw and shit, maybe some of the cops didn't want to engage based on that alone. Bottom line, I was mostly on my own, except for a few solid friends who championed my cause.

I felt that I had done all that I could. I had also caused so much trouble up there, I began to wonder if we were even able to operate safely anymore; it was time to go home and to stay there. Whatever we found of his, I had tried to bring it all back to a garage that I had rented near our apartment in Long Beach.

One night, months earlier, I was alone at my father's house. I was exhausted and had been up for days. I had sat down to do some heroin alone at the kitchen table and as I injected it, I passed out. I saw my father. I told him, "I've found your stuff. I got it back! I caught the thieves." He said, "It doesn't matter, it's okay." I stirred and awoke with the needle still in my arm. I was shocked. I had never done that before. I shook my arm violently flinging the needle across the floor. I believe I almost overdosed. It wasn't even all gone; had I done it all, I would be dead. I believe my father woke me up.

I had tried to fight the good fight. Oftentimes, I was no better than the drug-addicted thieves that robbed my father's house time and time again. I had done my best; I tried, as misguided as I was, to recover all of his stolen possessions. I thought I had to do something. Maybe I was trying to make up for the kind of nonexistent relationship we had. Was I, maybe, trying to finally gain approval? I don't really know, but I left the high desert, never to return.

At times, my very best was my very worst and it changed nothing.
—M.R.

LA RIOTS

It was Spring 1992, and I was staying at a hotel in downtown Long Beach during the time of the riots. I was standing with a few friends on the roof watching the city burn. Their cars were parked on the street, and one was out of gas and about to be towed away that day if we weren't able to move it. There was an empty gas can in the car, so Kristen and I grabbed it and I drove to get a gallon of gas. Long Beach was still under martial law, so we had to drive to Orange County to get gas. As we were going down Ocean Blvd, I noticed a security truck following us. He must've seen us with the gas can before we even began driving and became suspicious. After all, Los Angeles was burning. He followed us all the way to Belmont Shores, and he wasn't alone. I pulled over to ask him why he was following me, and as I got out of the car, I immediately realized that behind him were five or six black and whites. I assume he had called it in that he had seen a suspected arsonist. I was letting the cops have it because there was no reason to detain us for anything related to the fires. As the local news stations showed up, I'm sure due to the police activity over the radio, soon, we were being filmed, cuffed sitting on the curb as suspected arsonists on the evening news. We went to jail.

On the way to jail, I was yelling at the cops so badly, they pulled over and asked my girlfriend to please shut me up. I was mad at them for arresting her for a traffic warrant and felt they had better things to do at the time. She was able to calm me down and we were soon at the station and separated at intake. This began another odyssey of the wonderful world of city and county jails for me. In my lifetime, there had never been anything quite like the time of the riots. The holding cells, police stations, and jails were overflowing in capacity from the arrests. I was soon transferred to LA County jail at what must've been 4 am, caught in the chaos. It was already tense in the City, but by the time I arrived at County and rushed through intake with mostly people of color, for the next few days, I had to fight for my life. The dorms were standing room only, but we were expected to lay down and sleep. There was no room to stand, let alone lay down. Tempers were flaring and it was tight. I had a Jamaican guy tell me he hates everything white, even milk! We ended up fighting every time he and his friends saw me, all because I was white. I was fighting everyone because the sentiment in jail was, "Kill Whitey." The anger from the streets had overflowed on the inside due to the acquittal of the four white officers who beat Rodney King. I was in the middle of this chaos from that anger, and to them, I looked like I was part of the problem, but I was wearing county blues just like they were.

The riots lasted five days. There was over a billion dollars in damages and more than sixty people lost their lives. Ten people were shot by police and forty-four died of homicides and other consequences tied to the rioting. I felt like Los Angeles would never be the same again.

I was quickly entering the winter of my tenure as an addict. I had spent any royalties I received, used up any good favor, burned any bridges that somehow still existed. I had stolen, sold, or pawned anything I could get my hands on. My self-loathing and hand-crafted demise was almost complete. The one small thing that kept me going at all was my dog. Maybe deep inside it was something else, but I wasn't aware of it at all. I felt that Elvis was all I had left to live for. He was a living, breathing, non-judgmental soul that I was responsible for.

Trying to move away from all the chaos of the last year with mine and Kristen's addictions, the ever-present Long Beach Police Department, and the high desert circus, I had just been through, I needed to get away. The problem was that you can't run away from yourself. Once again, I was in trouble. It was September 1992, and I was pulled over in my El Camino in Long Beach for reasons I can't remember. The officer asked me if I had anything in the car and I told him that I had a gun behind the seat in a gun case. He proceeded to cuff me for his safety and retrieved the gun. He told me it was illegal to have it loaded and concealed. I said, "I told you where it was, I didn't hide it." When I asked him, "How do you carry yours?" he was less than pleased. He told me I should've had it in plain sight on the dash or center console. I said, "So, you wouldn't have pulled me over if my gun was on the dashboard?" He said, "That's the law." I was charged with a concealed and loaded firearm and received a year in County jail.

When I got out of jail, everything I had recovered from the high desert, all my father's things, were stolen from the garage in Long Beach. Kristen moved away from the apartment because things were so chaotic, and it had recently been raided. Around this time, we started having some problems and she pretty much shut down on me and began hanging around with a friend of ours at a place we both used to frequent to party. I sold him a little weed here and there. His name was Greg; he sold speed but was a nice enough guy. I generally liked him, that is until he started banging my girlfriend. I didn't see this coming, but I probably should have. We were pretty much flopping on people's couches, and that was no way to live.

ELVIS

My dog, Elvis, represented a connection to my ex-girlfriend, Claudia, who had passed away too young. The girl who apologized to me the night at the Observatory for hating me and claiming, "I killed her best friend," well she was referring to Claudia. The truth is, several years after we broke up, Claudia had passed. She was never able to kick her addiction and combined with her medical issues, I imagine that was what finally killed her. She loved Elvis dearly, so this added extra weight to me as his owner and caretaker. Flash forward after a breakup left me homeless again, it was just me and Elvis. I was able to find a great little bungalow in an old Mediterranean building in Long Beach. Yes, it was in the ghetto, but nonetheless, it was a safe place for me and Elvis to stay until I could figure out what was next. Maybe "safe place" is pushing it a little. It wasn't in a nice part of town, not even close, but I felt comfortable in that setting, after all, my bar was set pretty low. All I had to move in was a beat-up acoustic guitar, a trunk Ron had given me with some memorabilia, a few choice possessions, and a bit of clothing. No blanket, no pillow, or furniture, but Elvis and I had a roof over our heads.

The only problem was, dogs were not allowed, and I had neglected to tell the property manager that I had one. I felt I had no choice, but I figured I could talk to him the next day and ask if he could just give me a month. He could keep my security deposit, first and last, or whatever money was left while I sorted things out. Or maybe we could come to an agreement, which would allow me and Elvis to stay. My first night turned out to be the only night there. I slept on the floor with Elvis close to me. The next morning, I headed across town, on foot, which was well over a thirty-minute walk to the management office in hopes of coming to an agreement. Before I left, I put a Beware of Dog sign on the front door. I was completely telling on myself, but figured if anyone happened to show up, they wouldn't get hurt. Elvis was a good boy, but not to be messed with, so it was best for all concerned. When I arrived at the management office, the door was locked, and not a soul in sight, so I headed back across town to my apartment. I stopped on my way back to get a couple of cheeseburgers for me and Elvis. By the time I got back, there was a crowd of people standing in the front yard. I walked up and the neighbors told me that the landlord had gone inside my apartment and my dog bit him. Animal control had taken Elvis, my apartment was locked, and whatever I had was gone.

Homeless again within 24 hours, must be a record. Over the next few days, I tried to have Kristen, who was back in the picture now, and my mom try to get Elvis out, but they wouldn't release him. He was being held as a vicious dog pending a hearing. I couldn't appear, due to my warrants; I was wanted by the law. So, essentially my dog had a death sentence. I went down there, daily, pretending to look at strays. Since they didn't know what I looked like, they had no idea I was right under their noses. I could hear him barking from the back where they kept the vicious dogs or ones that got into trouble. I went so many times that Elvis lost his voice from barking, and I could no longer hear him, but I knew he was in there.

Having lost him, and by no fault of his own, since he was really just doing what he was supposed to be guarding our home and my possessions, I had to do something. He was a good boy, yes, he bit the landlord, but the landlord opened my door with a "Beware of Dog" sign" on it and walked inside. Maybe I have a twisted way of thinking, but it was mine and Elvis's house. He did what a dog is supposed to do when someone enters your home unannounced. Who opens a door with a "Beware of Dog" sign on it? I couldn't abandon him or leave him to be destroyed. It wasn't his fault. As bad as I was, fucked up on so many levels, I refused to let him pay for my mistakes or crimes. I tried everything I legally could within my power and had very few options at that point. So, I decided to break him out.

I began to case Animal Control like I imagine you would case a bank before a heist. It seemed that late at night there was only one person on duty, which surprised me. The problem was, he was being held in a secure section, like jail, where all the bad dogs were awaiting their cases or waiting to be put down. Although I couldn't hear or see him, I knew he was there. I found out that I knew someone who had knowledge of the way the place worked and confirmed Elvis was still inside. I'll leave him nameless, but I owe him a great debt. I was afraid I wouldn't be able to cut through the hardened steel fence and I didn't know how I would even get to him or how to get away. It was in Signal Hill, a place infamous for allegedly hanging somebody a few years earlier in their jail and the police station was near the pound. So, I was very concerned about getting caught.

Signal Hill is a small city backed up to Long Beach on one side and the 405 on the other. Industrial, mostly, in those days, so pretty quiet at night. I needed bolt cutters, so off to Home Depot for my first theft of the night. I walked in like I knew what I was doing and walked out with a pair of bolt cutters, straight to the car. I believe I was followed out the door, but for whatever reason he didn't pursue me. I didn't really think of myself as shoplifting, it was just necessary.

The idea was to wait late at night and call to Animal Control that there was a possum in my garage and it was scaring my children, please come out. I'd wait for the truck to leave then have Kristen drop me and a friend off to scale the fence. I would find my dog, cut him out, and somehow get his heavy little ass over the fence. Then out and meet Kristen, who was circling the neighborhood to pick us up out front. I told her if she saw any police or any action at all to drive away and leave us there. So, she dropped us off, we climbed the fence, jumped down, and ran into a second fence surrounding the vicious dog kennel. A Rottweiler was outside of his cage barking and going crazy until I jumped and landed in front of him. Luckily, he turned away and ran inside. Elvis was in the next kennel and came out through the door. He was excited as I cut away the fence to free him. The fence fell away like icicles, so it was easy, at that point, to get him out.

The next obstacle was lifting him over two more fences and he was very heavy. I got him up on my side of the fence, but it was all I could do to hold him up that high. He was like three bowling balls in a duffel bag, but I lifted him and thankfully my friend was able to catch him on the other side. I jumped that fence and was on to the next; we repeated the process and headed to the final gate. This gate was much taller, and I had no idea how we were going to get him over. It must have been nine feet tall and on a runner with a motor, so it remotely opened when trucks came in and out. Frustrated, standing there trying to find a way out, I somehow was able to kick it off the runner and slide it open just enough for all of us to escape. Amazingly, Kristen pulled up at the same time, we got in the car, and away we went. We did it! We saved Elvis.

He was all I had left, the one thing that didn't leave me and never would. The problem I faced now was, it would be obvious who stole the dog. Not many, if any, would steal a vicious dog from the pound. I was 6'4" with tattoos and long-ass straggly hair. You didn't have to be very smart or a super cop to find a tall, thin, strung-out-looking guy with a black and white dog walking around Long Beach. The obvious thing to do now was clear to me; it was time to dye Elvis a new color. That night we crashed at a friend's house and the next morning I walked to Thrifty's and bought two or three boxes of hair dye. I proceeded to tie Elvis to a fence post while I gave him a makeover. The problem was, dog hair doesn't take color like human hair. What does a dog do when they get wet? They shake, and he did, all over me. Whatever he didn't shake off covered one small chunk on his back, so I headed back to Thrifty's and bought more dye. He ended up looking like a camouflage rat. He was naturally all white with two black bandit spots on his face. In the end, the only white fur left was on his belly. Eventually, he was back to his beautiful color and perfect again. Within a few days, we were off to Morro Bay.

We spent a while in Morro Bay in another attempt to get away from the goings-on in Long Beach. We still found our way back despite the distance, it didn't change me or our bad habits. Later, I found out there was an article in The Press Telegram about an infamous dog breakout.

PRISON BOUND

This certain morning in February of '94 was just like any other. Wake up, get some dope so you can function, and start your day. We were in our new apartment so there was no phone hooked up yet. These were the days of pagers, not cell phones, and I needed a phone. Even though my old apartment was all but empty, the phone was still hooked up, so off I went just a few blocks away.

I ordered a forty from my connection, but when he arrived and we were making the exchange, he didn't have a forty, so he gave me two twenties. Same thing, right? It came with little baggies of coke which I didn't mess with, so I tossed them on the table. I didn't think anything of it and stuck the two twenties into my coin pocket. Normally I would've put them in my mouth, but I only had a few blocks to go. He headed out the door one way, and I exited a few minutes later and headed the other way on my mountain bike. I didn't get forty feet before I saw a Long Beach Police cruiser headed my way. I got out of the way by riding up onto the sidewalk, and he cut me off almost making me crash into his car. I was immediately grabbed from behind by a second unit I hadn't seen. I realized that I couldn't get to my pocket and the dope. I was FUCKED! One of the cops who was known in the area as "RoboCop" was a real dick with tightly cropped bleach blond hair. He was cleaning up the streets, one suburban dope fiend at a time. Hindsight being 20/20, maybe I was the asshole. I had a horrible sinking feeling as he questioned me and I knew I was fucked. I probably had warrants for FTA (failure to appear), but the dope, shit! Sure enough, he found it and proceeded to tell me that being on my bicycle constituted "transportation." Also, because my dope was in two packages it constituted "sales." There was a minimum mandatory sentence of three years. They were having a great time at my expense due to a new law. If I only had one package, it would have been a simple "possession."

In the end, I received formal probation for a period of three years following terms and conditions. 365 days in LA County jail with credit for 42 days; I'd be back out in 300 days or so. I was supposed to report to probation officers regularly, maintain an approved residence, do testing, and submit to search and seizure any time day or night, basically. I had a stiff and formal probation. With my mindset and behavior, I was destined to fail these circumstances, and I did.

A bench warrant was issued in February of '95 for my arrest. I was taken into custody and my probation was reinstated by September. I was ordered to serve an additional 180 days in County jail for violation. Actually, they gave me some kind of break considering all my previous arrests. In June of '96, a no-bail warrant was issued, and I was back on the inside once again. In November of '97, I was released and was staying with my friend, Adam, who was an heir to a large fortune. He was a bass player, rocker, and dope fiend. During my stay with him, he had to go back home to Ohio for the grand opening of a baseball stadium in honor of his grandfather. He had left his brand-new Suburban for me to use while he was away. One day, Jimbo, an old friend of ours and roadie for the band was pretty dope sick and called me. I was in a position to help him, so I took the Suburban and dropped off some dope so he could feel better. On my way back to Burbank, I passed a slower car as I exited the freeway. A CHP noticed my lane change and pulled me over. As I was being pulled over, I put the piece of dope I had in my mouth. The officer asked me what was in my mouth, and I said, "Nothing." I had swallowed it. I was wanted for failure to appear and for not meeting the terms of my probation. To top it off, I had a fake ID; they were immediately suspicious. It turned out the false ID name had a warrant as well, so I was taken out of the car and put into custody once again. I don't know how long it took me to give them my real name, but I imagine I did quickly because I realized no matter what, I was done. I was asking them to let me bring my friend's car home so it wouldn't be impounded, but that didn't happen and soon enough I was back in County jail awaiting another hearing. Count 1 to serve three years in any state prison. I was given credit for the days I already served on the two previous violations which meant I would serve under three years.

Here it is 1997 (*Exact date: November 12, 1997, my sober birthday*) and there I was, sick as a dog once again and for the last time. I was off the street and detoxing in County jail, undoubtedly on my way to State prison. I had talked to a couple "ambulance chasing" lawyers that I couldn't afford, but they couldn't help me anyway. There was no fighting my case. In court, they read the charges and mentioned the $30,000 dollar warrant I had for breaking my dog out of the pound. That charge was dismissed in the interest of justice, or so they said. I asked to be transferred forthwith, which means quickly. So, back to LA County jail, I went, waiting for the "Chain" and bus to take me to prison. I did most of my time in LA County. It was old and dirty, dangerous, and fucked and I had been there way too much. I had been to Orange County many times too and it was nicer, cleaner, and had better food.

The day had finally come, my name, along with many others, had been called; I was on my way to prison. In jail, it's always hurry up and wait, and getting bussed around always sucked, but this was going to be different. We were going to ride the "Green Goose" That's what the inmates, soon-to-be convicts, call the green CDC bus that transports you to the prison of their choice. I had been clean for weeks by this time and was thinking a little better. I still had a long way to go, and I was never very good with uncertainty. I think all the first-termers were nervous, I know I was. The prison transport was serious, they weren't playing. I think they wanted you to understand that right away. There was a steel cage in the bus where an armed CDC officer sat, keeping a watchful eye during the whole trip. We were going to Kern County where there are a ton of prisons. We were taken to Delano for reception. In reception, they grade you or rather figure out how many points you have. More points, worse prison, Level 1 being the easiest, Level 4 being the worst.

Delano was big, really big, and kind of intimidating. Walking down the large halls, it was loud and there were signs with "No warning shots fired," etc. It was no joke. We're not in Kansas anymore. The dorms were big also, well over a hundred beds. Nobody had been graded and separated yet by the severity of their crimes, so it was a bit of a mixed bag for sure, and a little squirrelly and potentially dangerous at times, it was rough. I still didn't feel good, I had lost everything, given it away, or traded it to get and stay high. What a fucking hole I had dug for myself. I had destroyed everything, lost everything.

The only communication I had was through letters which took weeks to get back and forth. I had written a letter to Mom and found out Elvis was gone. Adam had said he wandered away, but I believe he let him go. I asked my mom again through letters and weeks went by, to please search for Elvis, try the pound, put up signs, do whatever it took to find him; he was all I had left. Eventually and miraculously, I received a letter that she had found him at a pound. This meant my mom went to LA County in search of my dog for me. She paid the fines and was able to find a kennel where Elvis could stay. The guy running the place took such a liking to Elvis, that they hung out together in the office every day with his leash off, like buddies. Which is funny because Long Beach had dubbed him a vicious animal and was going to destroy him. I was lucky enough to pay for his housing through royalty checks still coming in from the band. As for Kristen, she was gone. I believe she was trying to get her life back on track and finally get off drugs. Together we didn't do each other any favors with our bad habits.

Soon after reception, I was sent to a community correction facility called Shafter. Probably because I didn't have any violent crimes, just low-level dope charges. Shafter wasn't what I would consider the main line. A larger prison could have thousands of inmates and more problems. But there were politics and rules and some of the normal goings on of dysfunctional men with too much time on their hands. But overall, I was able to stay out of trouble. I stayed free of issues that I may have suffered in a bigger institution. I followed directions, for the most part, and played by the rules and it worked out.

Somehow, I was elected as a representative for my dorm or zip code. This wasn't entirely appropriate because I was a first termer, so I had to learn on the fly. I was approached by the Hispanic shot caller of the dorm that one of the "Whites" was being harassed, bullied, and sex played in the kitchen, where they worked, by another "White" in the yard. He said it made us look bad and he wanted me to talk to the offender so they didn't have to. Also, because it would've possibly caused a much bigger problem, race against race possibly if he had intervened. I guess he thought I could pull the big dumbass offender aside and ask him to lay off the new soft guy. The next day in the yard, I saw the guy in question playing horseshoes. I knew a couple of skinheads from OC and asked them to watch my back while I went to go talk to this guy. Being who they are, they followed me instead of hanging back against the wall to watch me. This was dangerous as seen by the guards or others in the yard. Any group approaching another group looks like a potential altercation. I thought I was alone but continued to walk up to the guy and checked him. I told him to leave the kid alone, he denied any involvement. The next day I was summoned to a group of guys sitting by the weight pile. Turns out they were the shot-caller guys for their areas, the de facto leaders. Luckily, they understood I hadn't mastered prison etiquette yet and knew I was a first termer. I pleaded my case and they understood and said they would handle it, but in the future, no vigilante antics, and if I had a problem with anyone, come to the individual shot caller for that group area or car. It was a lesson learned. I wasn't going to make a habit out of coming here; I had better things to do.

For the first time in a long time, I was able to see clearly and realized I needed to make a massive change in my life. I had fucked off everyone and everything from my music career, bandmates, friends, and loved ones. I didn't mean to, but I had. I was in my late thirties by now and needed to do things differently. I realized that, maybe, I had one more chance. If I went back to my old behavior I would surely die or end up back in prison. At this point, I needed to prove to myself and others that I could change.

I steered clear of any politics on the yard and began reading and writing constantly. I stayed in contact with my family and decided to get my GED. I had left school so young, and with nothing but time, I decided to finish what I started. I found out there were classes at the facility, so I registered for school. I had begun this process at Wintersberg years ago in HB and found out I only had two more tests to complete. I was able to finish the classes in a short time and my first goal was complete. I was eating well and working out, probably for the first time in years. I knew I needed to start making plans for my release date. I never had any thought that the GED would matter in making it or not, nor was I impressed with the lower levels in school, but it was an accomplishment and the first of many, I had hoped.

I started making plans for how my life would look after prison. How I would live, where I would work, and how I would stay clean. I decided to stay out of Orange County and Long Beach, if possible. I would get any job I could, at first, and work my way up the ladder. My release date was getting nearer, and my family was very supportive. They visited me often and would bring me creature comforts from home. Shafter was nearly a three-hour drive for them to make each way. I appreciated this, and the support they showed. They probably had high hopes. The day I was finally released, I was driven back to a facility in downtown Los Angeles which was a disbursal center for convicts. It was actually an old apartment building next to the 110 freeway, but it was a California Department of Corrections (CDC) facility. You had to stay for a couple of weeks while it was decided where you would be sent. While I was there, they were remodeling the upstairs rooms and asked if I wanted to work; I said yes. So, when it was time for me to go, the officer took me in his office and said I was going to a halfway house. There were a couple of options and one was in Hollywood. This was a giant break for me. I asked If I could go there and, he said yes.

A lot of times my actions didn't match my intentions. — M.R.

SOBRIETY

Once I was free or somewhat free, it was expected that I would acclimate back into society and get a job. A lot of the guys failed and were taken back to prison immediately. I was familiar with Hollywood which could've been problematic for me based on my drug history, but I was determined to make a change. There was one AA meeting a week which was mandatory for me to attend and after two weeks you could go out to look for a job. Another perk was you could go out multiple times a week if you were going to a meeting. I seized on that and went to as many meetings as allowed. In the daytime, I walked around Hollywood and put out applications, looking for a job, while my nights were spent at meetings. I was there for a few months and picked up part-time work doing construction or whatever I could. Anything to keep me busy and out of the facility. My family continued to visit and were proud and hopeful of my progress. I was starting to get the program of sobriety. When it finally came time for me to leave the facility, still on parole, I found a studio apartment at 3rd and Manhattan in Korea Town, basically Hollywood.

Miraculously, I received a royalty check within two weeks of my departure which gave me enough money to pay for the rent. I had nothing but some clothes and shoes. There was a Murphy bed in my new little apartment. As soon as I moved in, my mom brought Elvis to me. He didn't recognize me at first, but after a few minutes he was happy to see me, I think he was just as happy as I was.

I landed a construction job on a luxury home that was being built somewhere near Will Rogers State Park in Santa Monica. I would take a bus every morning at 4:00am to a Starbucks and one of the construction workers would pick me up and drive me to the job site. Eventually I met a guy at one of the meetings that sold me a $500 truck. It looked exactly like you would picture a $500 truck to look. A chain holding the hood down and windows that didn't roll up, but it was mine.

By now, I had a fair amount of time being clean, even though I had acquired it in prison. Yes, there are drugs in prison, but I had made a decision to stay clean and sober and I did. It's suggested you have a sponsor during this time, someone to guide you through the steps of the twelve-step program, to make you accountable, and help you with simple things as well as major decisions. You really shouldn't do anything in your first years of sobriety without checking with your sponsor first. Their wisdom and experience are invaluable. After all, "Our good choices and best ideas" got us where we were.

I had a friend at the meetings who had over ten years clean and sober who became my sponsor, his name was Ron. Ron was also a co-owner of a coffee shop on Sunset Blvd. It was near the Guitar Center and other guitar shops and it was a familiar place to me where we would hang out, talk, and basically goof around before and after meetings. Ron and I would smoke cigarettes and talk a lot; we got along quite well. It was a place where the emphasis was more about sobriety, like a bar without the booze. We would go to meetings and play poker; we even started a business together. I checked with Ron and Mark Mahoney on pretty much every major life decision for a while. The owner of the company I worked for wasn't the nicest guy, and one day he wanted me to collect all the scraps of wood from the job site, cut them down, and deliver them to his home in Venice so he could use them in his fireplace. The next day was Saturday, and I got a call from him saying something to the effect of, "What the fuck is wrong with you? Are you fucking stupid? How am I supposed to fit these in my fireplace? They're supposed to be 6" long blah, blah, blah." This time I didn't wait to get any advice from my sponsor and responded with, "I don't know who the fuck you think you can talk to like that, but it's not me, fuck you, I quit." I called Ron immediately and told him the story and he agreed I didn't need to take that kind of abuse from a boss.

As fate would have it, I had a history with Ron that I didn't realize until much later. Come to find out, years earlier when I was escorted out of the house in Hollywood at gunpoint, he was one of the three guys there. He became such a good friend and confidant, we never discussed it, although I had put it together at one point. I don't know if he ever realized it was me, or maybe he did, but just didn't mention it. Oddly enough, that fucked up day removed me from a dangerous situation. I was still more dangerous to myself than anybody else could be, but it's still pretty weird.

Having a little time off now, I went to Sunset Strip to visit Mark at Tattoo Mania where he now worked. He was happy to see me and very pleased to know I was sober. I brought him up to date on my last few years, mostly the last few months, as he knew all too well how bad things were. He introduced me to the current crew at the shop and there was a piercer named Rick who was also the counter guy.

Things were picking up for piercers in the nineties and Tattoo Mania was no exception. Mark suggested to Rick that maybe he split a few shifts with me so he could be free to pierce more. Mark basically offered me a job. I started a few days a week and worked noon till closing. Usually in twelve-hour shifts, and most nights not getting home till 2:00 or 3:00 am. I was making a couple hundred dollars a day, cash. Mark saved my ass, I could pay my rent, not work for that asshole anymore, and be in a place that was comfortable, fun, and safe. Mark was watching out for me in an industry that I loved. I seemed to make a couple hundred a night from tips on good nights which paid my rent. I couldn't have been happier or luckier and all of it thanks to Mark!

Tattoo Mania was fun; you never knew who was coming in to get tattooed. Everyone from Angelina Jolie to Suge Knight, Jermaine Dupri, Nikki Sixx, and many more came through those doors. Mark's clientele was a who's who of actors, musicians, bikers, gangsters, and just characters in general. Mark had then and now style and class with a clever wit to match. The owner of the shop, Gil, was a character himself. He wasn't always around, he kind of came and went as he pleased.

By now I had been at Tattoo Mania for a while and Gill had learned of my experience with a clothing business and that I had a store at one point. Gill had an investor, Marco, and they wanted to start a tattoo-based clothing line. This was before the Ed Hardy Tattoo clothing line took off.

Gill wanted me to come to a meeting with his investor in Glendale. I thought this was a big opportunity to do something I had experience doing. A way to start making up for everything I fucked off. The meeting went well. I brought a business plan what kind of clothing I wanted to start with, and who our target audience might be. I had a plan, and they were impressed. I told them I needed a car and a warehouse and $700 a week to start. They rented me a car, we found a warehouse in the garment district in downtown LA, and we were off and running. I had two jobs now; things were looking up.

    I went to meetings almost every night. I wasn't forced, although I think my parole officer was pleased. Meetings were fun and I got it. I was finally starting to understand the program, the steps, and the fellowship. I understood, and more importantly, I believed, and even better, it was working. I had money, a job, and an apartment. For the first time in many years, I was free from the constant drive to get and use drugs. I was receiving all the gifts the 12-step program promised. I had been using something, whether it be alcohol, pot, coke, speed, or heroin since I was 11 or 12. Furthermore, I didn't know how to deal with my feelings, so I used. What a trip, I had been self-medicating for most of my life and had no idea. It's crazy that it was so simple, yet I didn't have a clue. I had been introduced to the program before and tried to go to meetings, but at the time I felt chased away by strict old-timers. I was yelled at for sharing at a meeting because I was a dope fiend. The old guard didn't see the connection, their intolerance showed when they said their meetings were for alcohol, period. I often wondered how many people didn't make it back. This time I was getting it and I wouldn't be chased away. Things had changed, I had somehow survived against all odds, and despite myself and my self-destructive behavior, I was still here. I was grateful for all the gifts I had been given. I had another chance, at the very least, to survive, and if I was lucky, maybe even to thrive and play in band again. But even if that wasn't in the cards, just having an apartment, my dog, and a job, to not wake up sick or being a slave to the powder, the pill, or the needle was better than before. I was given a second chance. I needed to make the most of it, and one thing they teach you is to help the newcomer, which I did. Whenever and wherever I could, even if it was just reaching out at a meeting.

One day at work I was talking to Mark about the program. He said we help all kinds of people we don't even know, what about the people we do know who are still out there? I agreed, but didn't quite follow him, who was he talking about? He was talking about Ron Emory. Ron had fallen just as badly as I had, but just a little later. I saw Ron from time to time. We still hung out before I went to prison and he was pretty fucked up too. We both were at the time, but now I had been clean for quite a while. To be truthful, longer than I had ever been in my whole life. I was active in recovery and trying to help other addicts who were still suffering. It's part of what you were supposed to do, Mark was right.

We had a friend, Rod, who worked with or at Impact, a tough rehabilitation place in Pasadena. I also knew Rod, he was funny and kind of wild, but very serious about his job. Mark talked to Rod, and he got Ron a bed, a free bed. All Ron had to do was complete the program. Oh yeah, and consent to go to rehab, and at this point, I hadn't spoken to him yet. I made a couple of calls and received a call back from Ron. I said, "What's up?" His response was always the same as it had been with me, hustling to stay well, sick every day, struggling to stay alive. As we spoke this time, I pitched it to Ron from my heart. I know he heard I was sober, but I doubt he believed it. Anyway, I told him he had one shot and Mark had called a friend who arranged for him to have a free bed in Impact. I explained that this was a big deal, and he should take this offer. I said, "This may be your last chance." Ron agreed, wow!

Next, I had to pick him up in OC and bring him to Korea Town to my apartment until we could get him into Impact. He took a train to downtown LA where I picked him up. A problem arose when I found out his bed wasn't ready. I had Ron sleep on the couch in my studio apartment with Elvis and me. Each day I took him to work with me in downtown to my warehouse. I let him sweep the warehouse to keep him busy. I gave him $20 dollars a day so he could stay well until Impact was able to take him in and help him detox. He either used in my apartment bathroom or the bathroom at the warehouse. I didn't want to let him out of my sight until he was safe at Impact. Funny thing is, he later told me he used to watch me sleeping. He had known me for so long, it was hard for him to believe I wasn't using, and I was able to sleep. Oddly enough, I didn't feel anything when Ron got and used dope in my presence. I only felt that it was keeping him on ice until he could enter the rehab. Amazingly it seemed my own obsession had been removed.

A few days after his stay with me, I took him to Impact. He was so beat up they feared for his heath and wouldn't take him in his current condition. He wanted it so bad, and his story was so compelling, the director agreed to hold a bed for him. He could move in after a medical detox and some attention to his wounds, so I dropped him at the hospital with high hopes. Ron became a rockstar at Impact. He followed directions, worked a program, held a job on site, and helped with newcomers. Eventually he graduated and moved to a sober living house in Marina Del Rey where he became house manager. Ron has been clean and sober 22 years as of 2021.

I've been part of the problem and I've been part of the solution during my life. As luck would have it, my addiction was interrupted by a stay in prison where I had time to reflect and think about my future. Not all are so lucky.

My personal journey, like most I would imagine, has been peppered with success and failure. I was truly my own worst enemy, but through it all, somehow, I survived in no small part to finding programs of recovery. In my opinion, Jack, Ron, Greg, and I owe our current lives to the 12 step program. I have 24 years clean and sober as of November 12, 1997.

The only way I've learned to do the right thing is by doing the wrong thing too many times. — M.R.

SOCIAL CHAOS & TATTOOING

Probably the true rebirth of the band was when we were asked to play an art show in Santa Monica; it was 1999. John Doe was involved. He is a great guy and a super talent and seemingly tolerant, or at least understanding of the beach punks and our antics over the years. In my opinion, the early Hollywood scene was more artistic, whereas we, the beach punks, were more literal or rather physical. Jack was contacted by John to see if he would play a few songs at the art exhibition. At the time, the band hadn't been together in many years, and Jack was asked to play with a backup band which he declined, saying that would be weird. Instead, Jack reconnected with Ron and me after my stint in prison. For the first time in a long time, both Ron and I were clean for longer than we had been ever before in our lives. We added Jay O'Brian on drums after Todd's passing in 1999 of a brain aneurism.

I rented a room at a local studio in Hollywood with a small amp and a cassette recorder. I turned the PA on and put the mic next to the boom box. I played along to our songs to try to practice and get back into the groove a little bit. I don't recall us rehearing at all as a band for this show. This speaks to the way we have played forever. Today, living in different states, we just show up and play. The night of the show was a who's who of punk rock personalities. It was great to see so many people I hadn't seen in years. Just to be part of it all was amazing. When it was our turn to play, we got on stage and it was just like old times. We started the first song and the crowd went wild. It was chaos, like being in the eye of the storm. The lighting trellis fell, a bottle was broken, drinks were spilled, and amps were being knocked over. Equipment was broken and blood was shed when a bouncer caught a stray elbow chasing someone across the small stage. It was a perfect show, just like old times. We were reborn! As we left the small stage, John Doe said, "Nice Set." I imagine it was in a tongue-in-cheek kind of way. I let out little laugh; it was fun. That's how it was supposed to be.

We received a parting gift of a glitter coated vinyl record glued to a piece of plywood for our outstanding achievements in punk rock. Our crew member and lifelong friend, Bobby Sepulveda, still has the award to this day. I believe this started us all thinking maybe we can do this again. And more importantly, Jack might have started thinking he could trust us enough to play with us again. After all, it was Ron and I that had something to prove. This was Ron's first show that he played clean and sober. We had to regain Jack's trust, as he had been staying out of trouble for a while. Let's not pretend Jack wasn't still being Jack, but he had successfully been clean and sober for over a decade. Ron and I still had a lot to learn.

Out of the blue in the summer of 1999, an opportunity came up for a big tour, Social Chaos. Gil and his partner/investor, Marco were still fighting over the clothing line, and here I was in the middle with one foot in each side, at this point. I still wanted to be part of the tattoo world, but I also had a stake in the clothing business. I couldn't pick one side or the other. I couldn't cut my throat and choose the investor over Gil. The tattoo world was different then, and not just business, there was a certain etiquette of loyalty. Even though Mark was my guy, I didn't want to offend Gil despite having several accounts ready to go. Following a successful launch of the Tattoo Mania clothing line at the NY trade show, I hung up the garment bag in my closet and tried to prepare for my first nationwide tour in years.

Jack had approached us with an offer we had received for a tour, and it sounded good, and the money was solid. I hadn't toured in years, but I still tried to play regularly even if it was only on my couch. I hadn't played in a band for a long time. The tour was called Social Chaos; it was billed as "Anarchy in North America Tour '99" with TSOL, The Business, D.O.A., U.K. Subs, Murphy's Law, Anti Heroes, Gang Green, Sloppy Seconds, Chelsea, Vice Squad, Etc.

Ron and I were both quite new in sobriety compared to Jack. In Jack's eyes I'm sure we must have seemed pretty risky, although I had over a year, almost two clean, and to me it seemed like a lot of time. To Jack we were unproven and hadn't been exposed to the world on a large scale for a while, so the jury was still out in his mind, I'm guessing. We toured in a motorhome with Bobby as our main tech who was Jack's guy at the time. Bobby was a little shyster and you just had to love him; he works for Diana Ross now. Bobby would collect the merchandise money and was instructed to walk past us and not give us any information on how we did. The money went straight to Jack for accounting purposes. In all fairness, Jack had been active and pretty successful during the years that Ron and I were still out running amuck, destroying our lives. We bickered and complained a little about it, but as the tour went on Jack learned to trust us a little more, and I mean "a little."

The bigger problem was the number of bands on the tour and the amount of money promised to each band by the promoter. There were a lot of great bands on the tour, so oftentimes when something seems too good to be true, it is too good to be true. The challenge was getting to the promotor first after each show to get paid, and that was my job. All while the other bands were in line to collect as well. Nobody was getting the money they were promised. I don't know if Jack picked me to be the collector because I just got out of prison or simply because he's just never been the one to want to soil his hands with the money. Every town, every show, every new date was a struggle to get paid. There were too many mouths to feed and not enough food. By the time the tour made it to Seattle with a $25 all ages ticket, which was a good deal, a few of the bands, Murphy's Law, DRI, and Gang Green had dropped out.

The tour continued with us making the best of every situation and learning to play as a band again. Jack hadn't missed a beat during our absence and had a few projects under his belt. On the other hand, I would imagine I was a little rusty, but I'm sure Ron probably killed it. Nothing like a few shows in rapid succession to knock out any of the cobwebs. I don't remember if we completed the tour or if it collapsed, but I do know this is what started us back up again.

It was 1999 and after a month of shows, the tour was over. I was back at work at Gil Montes' Tattoo Mania which became a life changing place for me. While working as a helper there, I had started expressing an interest in tattooing, and only with Mark's blessing, was I allowed and encouraged to do so. So, talks with Mark and some of the other artists there started to take on a whole different feel. Now I was being given tips and instruction, and once in a while Freddie Negrete or one of the guys would throw me a small tattoo. It became clear to me, I wanted to do more.

Mark said I should learn it all and wanted me to go to a shop on Hollywood Blvd called Ink Freaks. Tattoo Mania wasn't a beginner's shop after all, so I took his advice and Duel at Ink Freaks took me under his wing. I recall learning most of the nuts and bolts of tattooing from Duel. Tattooing back then wasn't just about being an artist. You had to learn how to watercolor, paint flash, build machines, make needles, mix pigment, and so on. Mark's amazing talent, in my opinion, came from the understanding of what his client wanted, or rather needed, and the overall nuance of design. He was more charismatic than any other tattooist I knew of, with a persona like no one else. In other words, he was far above showing me the rudimentary basics of tattooing 101.

The daily scene had been fun on at the Sunset Strip. Always busy and wildly crazy. Clubs were cracking, and I still had the energy to work endless hours. The clothing line was a bust, as Gil and Marco were never able to reconcile their differences. Somewhere around this time, Gil had decided to sell his shop and had made a deal with Mark to buy it. Mark went to Boston to secure the funds, but when he returned, he found out Gil had sold the shop for a higher number to Rocco, who was another tattoo shop owner who desperately wanted a spot on the Sunset Strip. This created a ton of tension between Gil, Rocco, and Mark. Over the next year or so, it became more and more tense to work there with Gil gone and the new owner trying to run things. Mark had decided to open his own shop and found a location on the Sunset Strip a couple blocks down and across from the Key Club. He had planned to take a good amount of the crew along with him, including Freddy and Isaiah.

Due to the competitive nature of the tattoo industry, the move and building of the new shop was kept secret up until the day it opened. Ron and Gia Emory did a lot of the work on the interior. In fact, Ron pretty much built the shop. It had a custom vibe with an old school feel. Mark had classic and impeccable taste, and the shop reflected this with features of an era gone by. There was even a pool table in the front lobby that still remains today. Mark had me get the neon Shamrock signs made for the front windows that still hang there today. In 2001, "The World-Famous Shamrock Social Club" opened its doors and remains an iconic place on the Sunset Strip.

By this time, I had been tattooing four days a week at Big Brian's "In The Skin Tattoo" in Pasadena and it was a good shop in a good neighborhood compared to Hollywood Blvd. I had always kept my relationship with Shamrock, so while working there, Mark had given me one permanent day a week tattooing at Shamrock. It was a great place to be during that time in Hollywood and as Mark would say, *"Where the elite and the underworld meet."*

BACK TO PUNK ROCK

I remember playing a handful of shows between 1999 and 2001. Some of the stand outs, to me, were playing with, The Business, Murphy's Law, UK Subs, NOFX, The Offspring, Social Distortion, and Pennywise at Irvine Meadows. We were on The Vans Warped Tour on July 1, 2000 at Pier 30/32 in San Francisco with, Green Day, NOFX, and Long Beach Dub All Stars.

Jack got us signed by Nitro records, who was owned by Dexter Holland and bassist Greg Kriesel of The Offspring. We rented a lock out room in a basement studio complex in Long Beach and started writing. We worked almost every night, trying to come up with our first new record in years. Jack would come and go as we tried to grind out the songs for the new record. We wrote a lot of songs and even a few we really liked. As I remember, Jack wasn't sold on the first batch of songs; he just wasn't feeling it yet. Ron and I were a little frustrated, but Jack knew what he wanted and what he didn't, so we kept working and eventually ended up with 12 songs. We were also going to be reunited with our old friend and producer of *Dance with Me*, *Weathered Statues*, and *Beneath the Shadows*, Thom Wilson (RIP).

We recorded at Track Record in North Hollywood. The name of the album would be *Disappear*. It was great and completely natural to work with Thom again, and in all fairness, I was along for the ride and trying to do my part. I hadn't been in the studio for a long time, so I couldn't have been happier about this chance again. We played two shows at Universal Amphitheater opening for The Offspring, which began a tour with them and a pop punk rock band, Millencolin. The tour was ten dates beginning in July of 2001 and finishing in September of 2002. A major highlight on that tour was playing Inland Invasion at Glen Helen Blockbuster Pavilion with 65,000 fans and an insane lineup of bands that included, The Offspring, Bad Religion, Blink 182, Social Distortion, Sex Pistols, The Dammed, Pennywise, X, The Circle Jerks, Buzzcocks, TSOL, The Distillers, Adolescents, GBH, The Vandals, and Unwritten Law.

Because I got out of prison, off meth and heroin, sober and staying clean, Kristen and I eventually were able to meet back up. She had got off heroin, had an apartment and a job, but she was still on methadone. As we talked, she told me she was lowering her dose each week trying to finally get off everything. Not many people ever get completely off methadone, she was the only woman at her facility to completely detox and not relapse. We would meet up with sober friends, have coffee, hang out, and go to meetings. One thing led to another, and I broke it off with the girl I was dating and eventually got back with Kristen. By this time, she was totally clean and sober, and things were looking up.

Standing outside her apartment in Santa Monica watching the sky, there was not one airplane in sight. It was surreal, other worldly, like nothing we had ever experienced before. It was 9/11 and the world stopped. Although I never planned on getting married, that's when I proposed to her, and she accepted. We were married at her family's ranch, went to Vegas for our honeymoon, and went right back to life at home in Santa Monica. I thought we were happy, but there were still problems somewhere deep inside. I was working long hours, playing with the band, and played cards too much, often late into the night. She had her own issues which left her looking for attention elsewhere. Clearly that doesn't happen if you're happy at home. I had either just got home or was preparing for a big show, or both, but something had changed, and it was over. I didn't realize it right away, and I didn't handle it very well either. We were married for around two years.

In September of 2002, TSOL headlined a show at the House of Blues on the Sunset Strip. Unfortunately, a fight broke out and a shooting occurred. It was reported to be a racially motivated attack. This was bad on so many levels, people were hurt and terrified. We had finally played at a national venue, and it was over just like that. The result was TSOL being banned and sued. We had sold out two nights and the second night was cancelled. We were exonerated of any involvement, but nevertheless the damage was done.

By 2003 Billy Blaze replaced Jay O'Brian on drums for our release of *Divided We Stand* which also featured the return of Greg Kuehn on keyboards and was produced by David Bianco. In support of this release, we went to Europe in June of 2003 for The Deconstruction Tour, headlined by NOFX. Also, on the bill was, Thrice, Strung Out, Boy Set Fire, The Real McKenzies, and Bouncing Souls. We also played the Download festival on one stop of the tour at Castle Donington, England. It was The Iron Maiden Festival, and to Todd it was the Holy Grail! To our surprise, Metallica who wasn't even on the bill, was inserted right before us. Are you kidding me? They landed in a helicopter and walked on stage before our set with their security pushing people, including me, out of the way.

The tour was fun and going overseas was interesting and exciting. The only real problem was, we shared a double decker sleeper bus with some of the tour's action sports skaters and BMX kids. By kids, I mean they were much younger than us and acted like children. One and all thought they were in Led Zeppelin and the bus was their hotel room. Night after night they partied all night, broke bottles, and barfed somewhere in the bus, usually on one of the community couches in the downstairs lounge. Jack asked nicely for them to shut it down a few times with little or no change. Finally, he had enough and verbally gave them both barrels, also threatening if he had to wake me up, they wouldn't like it. I personally think he's scarier than me when he is pissed off, but either way this seemed to finally work, and they quieted down a little. A downside for me was that we didn't have our own vehicle to venture out. Adventures on tour is what we're all about and we couldn't really go anywhere under the circumstances.

In 2004 Anthony "Tiny" Biuso replaced Billy Blaze on drums. It was usually my job to try out drummers, so I had booked time at the same studio in Hollywood where I rehearsed alone before our first show that led to us reforming. I had given Tiny a list of songs to rehearse before his audition. He drove up in a pickup truck, and I helped him load in his equipment. He proceeded to set up his drum kit and not only did he know the songs, he claimed he knew *all* of the songs that I had given him to rehearse. He only had a few days to learn these, so I was very surprised and impressed given the short amount of time and that he probably didn't know any of them prior. We set up and made small talk, as I was just trying to get to know him. He was very matter of fact and confident, so in a short while we were ready to play. I asked him what he wanted to do, and he said, "Any of them." I picked a song, and he nailed it first time. We picked another song, and again he nailed it, first try. I picked a third and he, once again, nailed it. I don't believe we did more than five songs in total, and I asked him, "You know the songs?" He said, "Yeah, I got it." I said, "That's great, you got the job!" Come to find out years later, he was a little shocked and dismayed that we rehearsed as little as we did.

During 2005, with Tiny on drums, we released *Live in Hawaii*, *Who's Screwing Who*, and a re-recorded *Divided We Stand*. In 2006, we played two shows billed as our "Farewell Shows," as if we were retiring. I don't even remember why it was billed this way, maybe Jack was done again. More likely it was Bobby's idea as a ruse to sell out both nights and get us a large guarantee. It was two nights at The Vault in Long Beach, the band's original home turf. Bobby arranged the shows, as I recall, and the line-up included on one or both nights, 45 Grave, Smut Peddlers, The Crowd, The Dead Reagan Tour, The Detours, DI, and Manic Hispanic.

Our retirement seemed to be short-lived. By 2007, we were playing live again, and in 2008 we were back in the studio laying down tracks for *Life Liberty* and *The Pursuit of Free Downloads* for Bob Hurley of Hurley International. We had known Bob since we were all kids. Bob was a big fan and wildly successful. He wanted to give back and this time he did by gifting free music to his customers. The album was also referred to as our 30th Anniversary album, produced by David Bianco once again. At the time, I don't believe there were any hard copies made; all you had to do was download this, the record was free.

Around this time, I had been living with and dating a new girlfriend, Tatianna for a couple of years, actually a friend of mine's ex-girlfriend. She had been good for me in some ways, helping me financially, and helped me to behave a little more like an adult. On a trip to Vegas, most likely centered around her job which was opening a shop in Caesars, we decided to get married. It was the day before her birthday, and she had wanted to get married; it was her thing, to be married, and I was not her first husband. For me, it was the most adult relationship I had so far, and it seemed like the right thing to do. She was independent, successful, and completely comfortable with my schedule of being away half the week, splitting my time between LA and Vegas, and touring. We had two dogs and a house on a hill, I was doing well at the tattoo shop, and everything seemed fine. That being said, I was never trying to get married once, and now I'm married twice. Fast forward eight to ten years later and cracks started to show in the relationship. I backed her to take her dream job in New York, telling her I would manage everything on the home front. At first, it was hard for her to be away, and she wanted to come home. But as she became more comfortable, I noticed a change. Ultimately things went from bad to worse and it had become obvious she was cheating, so by the time her stint in New York was over, so was our marriage.

TSOL did some dates on the Vans Warped Tour in 2009, and also did a two-week southwest tour, headlining, which started in Pomona at The Glass House. We toured most of Texas, had some shows in Arizona, and finished in Los Angeles, totaling fourteen shows in seventeen days.

HART & HUNTINGTON

Mark Mahoney oftentimes helped me with major decisions and just life in general. One day, Clark North, a tattoo artist at Hart & Huntington in Las Vegas approached Mark and asked if they could come down to Shamrock. Clark, being from California, viewed Shamrock as a classic old tattoo shop; he had apprenticed with Rick Walters. He wanted to bring an apprentice to Shamrock and film an episode for their new show, *Inked*. They wanted to bring him on a night when we were all there working. The crew was Rick Walters, Small Paul, Mark, Freddy, Boo Boo (Isaiah Negrete, RIP), and me. Mark agreed and they showed up with a film crew. Clark, Mooch the manager, and Dizzle the apprentice, who was terrified I imagine. We had a great time teasing Dizzle, putting pressure on him, tormenting him lightly. At one point Rick Walters suggested that Dizzle should actually do a tattoo. We were wondering on who. We didn't have anyone to tattoo, Rick said, "Tattoo me!" I think Dizzle almost fainted at that point, but we set up a station so he could tattoo Rick. The absolute terror we saw in his eyes was unparalleled. I can't even imagine how scared he must've been with all of us hovering over his shoulder, correcting his every movement, and the simple fact, alone, that he was tattooing an industry legend; we all laughed and had a good time. *Inked* was the first tattoo show of its kind and changed everything for good and bad.

Clark and I had known each other as kids, and we lived in the same housing tract in Huntington Beach. During the time he was at Shamrock to film the episode, he and I spoke lightly about tattooing in Vegas. I showed some interest, and less than a week later, he contacted Mark for his approval to offer me a job. This was the proper etiquette at the time. I'm grateful that Mark decided to allow me to go because working in the shop in Las Vegas changed my life, monetarily, for the better. Although

I do miss Hollywood, Mark, and the experience and family that Shamrock is and was. Shamrock is a different kind of shop than anywhere else I've ever worked.

I was on board and excited for the opportunity that lay ahead. That being said, it must have taken a year to finally get a shift of my own at Hart & Huntington. I basically worked overflow and taking any open shift available if someone hadn't already snatched it up. Finally, I was offered a shift of my own, a Tuesday, one day a week, so I accepted. Mooch couldn't believe that I would take this one day. This meant I would commute from Los Angeles to Las Vegas for the spot.

The guys at Hart & Huntington were killing it. Easily making six figures for the best artists and probably benefiting from the TV show, *Inked*. Hart & Huntington was also one of the first shops able to raise pricing for a quality tattoo. I wasn't a particularly fast tattooist, as I wasn't trying to make a mistake or do a bad tattoo. For me, even tattooing one day a week at a slower pace was worth the time. I was still able to make $500 a shift. I was committed and it was about to pay off. A shift would open up here and there, and soon I was working five full time spots a week. Corporate, as they like to call themselves, was always easy going and supportive. Mooch, Jay, and Big B were my main points of contact, and once in a while, Carey would come around. It was great working with all those guys.

At first, I was staying in hotels once a week and driving rental cars back and forth. I was able to afford this and make it worthwhile at the time. A rare rude awakening came when a convention would be in town and there were no hotel rooms available, so I would have to sleep in my car. Eventually I rented an efficiency apartment right off the freeway near South Point Casino. It was $600 a month and had a microwave and a Murphy bed. I brought bedding from home and bought my first flat screen TV, which was a big deal at the time. After a year or so working at the shop, I was making more money and decided to upgrade to a nicer apartment. I moved to a gated community in Silverado Ranch with granite counter tops, washer and dryer, and fireplace. It was nicer, safer, and still only around $1,000 a month. At this point, I was making good money.

The original shop was located at the Palms in 2004, however I don't believe the Maloof brothers were ever fans of tattooing. To my knowledge, our management was in discussions, at some point, to move our shop to the Hard Rock Casino. The Hard Rock was being renovated and they thought we would be a good fit so we opened up there in 2009. At first, we didn't seem to be as busy, in my opinion, maybe due to people unaware of our move. For me personally, it was like going to work at a playground. Every door, wall, room, and inch of the Casino covered in rock-n-roll memorabilia. Showing up to work with big bands on site doing their residency or a one-night show was something I didn't take for granted. I enjoyed my time at the Hard Rock; it was and will always be legendary. There was a lot of history there, including the death of legendary bass player John Entwistle of The Who. One day before The Who was to set out on tour, he died of a heart attack in his hotel room. It's widely known that this was brought on by his use of cocaine. At any rate, being a giant fan of rock and music in general the Hard Rock will always be a memorable place for me.

The Hard Rock Hotel closed its doors in 2020 when it was purchased by Sir Richard Branson and would soon become Virgin Casino. Hart & Huntington had plans to open back up after the remodel, but ultimately, we relocated to Caesar's Palace where we remain today.

During my time with Hart & Huntington I would drive back and forth from LV to LA hundreds of times. I burned through half a dozen cars, have been married and divorced, done thousands of tattoos, and toured the world with TSOL. I still have a relationship with Hart & Huntington today, nearly twenty years later. I'm lucky to work among such talented artists. I consider them friends and extended family. BJ my manager, Sandy, the assistant manager and artists Lacey, Eric, Shaun, Ron, and Damien, and more recently, Christian and Carlos.

A NEW DECADE

We embarked on a European tour with Pennywise in January of 2011. Touring with them was always crazy and fun. Randy, the bassist, is an old friend and Fletcher is a dear friend and one of our biggest fans, not to mention a wild man. I actually did a TSOL tattoo on his wrist. His antics on tour were legendary and not all for good reasons. Although at this point in his life he was more subdued. I think it helped that he got off the hard alcohol, but still seems to get into trouble from time to time. In early June, we played a night at the Key Club with Youth Brigade where a massive riot broke out when the club had sold out and the crowd was overflowing into the street. Cops showed up and kids were throwing bottles and rocks. Luckily, I parked across the street at Shamrock, and I remember getting out right when the shit hit the fan. People were stuck inside the club in what probably felt life forever, including Youth Brigade.

We toured all of June through the US and played the East Coast for the first time in six years. In March 2013, we played the Musink Festival with Bad Religion, Pennywise, Lag Wagon, Reverend Horton Heat, Guttermouth, Lemmy, and Two Bags. Musink was where my two worlds collided. As well as seeing all my friends and colleagues from the tattoo industry, I had all the punk bands from my world coming together making it a busy and fun filled day, the bonus being it was held in Orange County. Originally Musink began as a project of Bill Hardy who is an old friend and has been involved in the music scene as long as I can remember. Today with the collaboration of Travis Barker and SGE, it's evolved by adding a rad car show and is one of, if not the most, alluring tattoo and music festivals in the world.

We did a South American tour in June of 2013 playing, Buenos Aires, Sao Paulo, Curitiba, Porto Alegre, and Florianopolis. Cesar Carpanez was a promoter in South America who had a lot of success with Pennywise, among others. He was the "go to" guy for South America. He traveled with us during the whole tour because of distance and safety factors. We flew from date to date, due to the drives being long and not through the safest of areas. South America was beautiful and amazing. We finished in Florianopolis, which is a world-famous surf spot, not unlike the North Shore of Hawaii. It was a great opportunity and a blessing to see South America, and I'm grateful to Caesar for taking us.

We went on to play Riot Fest in Chicago in September 2013. 110,000 people with multiple stages with some great bands, Dinosaur Jr., Flag, Blondie, Public Enemy, X, Violent Femmes, Blink 182, just to name a few. One of the highlights, for me, was getting to see Blondie from backstage. Directly following that show, we did an East Coast tour with Flag. In my opinion, Flag was the only "real" Black Flag still playing. Keith Morris was the singer, although later Henry Rollins may have been more popular singer to some fans, but to us, Keith and Black Flag were one in the same. By 2014 we were offered an East Coast tour with The Damned and The Briefs. I think it's safe to say The Dammed was, bar none, TSOL's favorite band, so the chance to be support on this tour was above and beyond. All the members of The Dammed were really nice guys, kind and gracious, and I feel very lucky to have shared a stage with some of our earliest heroes; Todd would've been proud.

In October of 2015, we played the second stage at It's Not Dead Fest in San Bernadino. The one-day event was jammed packed with 35 punk bands. It was a who's who of all stars including, Bad Religion, Pennywise, Descendants, Fishbone, NOFX, The Vandals, and once again we shared a stage with, Adolescents, Manic Hispanic, Agent Orange, and The Dickies, among others. We continued to play shows through 2016 and in 2017. Gary Tovar and Paul Tollett offered us a spot at Coachella for the first time. This was a huge opportunity for us to promote our new album, *The Trigger Complex*. Although we didn't have a drummer at the time, the noteworthy thing about this show was Max from Fidlar, also Greg Kuehn's son, played drums for us. We also played The Vans Warped Tour around this time, possibly the last one. We had a long history with Kevin Lyman from the music industry. He's best known as the creator and founder of the event.

We had just lost a drummer, so Rise Records had hooked us up with someone to fill in on our upcoming tour. But after a two-song rehearsal with Ron and I, it was over. He just couldn't keep up, so I called Jack and said, "We're fucked!" Jack put it out on social media with my number, and I received a call from Antonio two days before we were leaving on tour. I wasn't very nice, as I recall; I had no time to fuck around. I said, "Can you play, can you keep time?" He said he could, so I told him to meet us at the studio and after 15 minutes, we told him, "You have the job, we will be leaving in two days," handed him the set list, and said, "Learn it!" He did and has been with us ever since. He's been a great addition to the band, easy to get along with, soft spoken, eager to play, and hard working.

So, we had a new drummer as of May 2017. As the story goes, Antonio was my mailman before he joined the band. Jack likes to tell it like this, "Antonio was delivering mail to Mike and looked through his window and saw a TSOL poster on his wall." Jack paints it out to be creepy that Antonio was looking through my window. The fact is, there were quite a few framed TSOL posters on the wall openly visible from the mailbox.

We went on to do a few East Coast dates in December with The Bouncing Souls. They're great guys and a great band. The bassist, Brian Kienlen is a fellow tattooist and owns a successful shop on the East Coast (Jersey Shore.) He was gracious enough to let us stay at his house when we were there on tour. The following spring, we played shows with the Dead Kennedys in Chicago, IL, Ohio, Michigan, Missouri, and Pennsylvania. We also played Creepy Fest, a one-off event in New Orleans, then The Brak Rock Echo Fest in Belgium.

In the summer of 2018, we were back in the states and playing a handful of shows at bars and clubs on the West Coast. During a two-night stint at Marty's in Newport Beach, I met Tracy. She's a Huntington Beach girl who had known Jack for years, from his time in Tender Fury. At the time, I was nearing the end of my divorce, and Tracy had been divorced the year prior. Neither one of us were expecting to meet one another. I was in the middle of my usual hustle, collecting the money after the show, when I saw Tracy with Robin Grisham. I introduced myself to her in the tiny backstage room, as everyone was packing up to leave. I walked them out to her car and we exchanged a sideways hug. Later, Tracy said during the show, Robin referred to the moment as "A Parallel Universe."

Jack was surprised we had never met in the past thirty years. We later learned we were in the same place at the same time on more than one occasion, including a night that involved a stop at the hotel where she worked in the 80s. I was meeting Slash after one of their sold out shows at Pacific Amphitheater to drop him a little piece of dope. My friend and later roadie to the stars, Jimbo, was with me. GNR happened to be staying at the hotel where I later found out Tracy worked and was there that night. She was working in the hotel café while I was doing a favor. I also soon found out during one of our reunion shows, billed as "Superficial Love" in '91 at UC Irvine, a PA system was knocked down into the crowd and Tracy was injured quite badly. That was the only time she saw me play before the night we met.

The morning after the show, the band had a record signing lined up at an ice cream shop in Orange County. She came with Robin, and we exchanged a hello and a hug. Immediately following, I had to catch a flight to our next show, but there was a miscommunication between Jack and me and instead of leaving from Orange County, he booked me leaving from Las Vegas. I had to hightail it back that night straight to the airport in Vegas to catch my first flight, which I missed by 15 minutes. The lady at the counter said she could get me there for another $100 on top of a new ticket somewhere between $300 and $400. Mind you, I forfeited the already purchased ticket for my missed flight. Oh, and this flight would only be four stops. I flew all day and crisscrossed the nation, finally arriving in Texas in the early evening. After deplaning four times, hustling to the farthest terminal each time for the next flight, I somehow caught up to the band in time for the drive to the show. The day I flew home to Las Vegas, I called Tracy and told her I was thinking about driving to see her and what did she think? She said, "Come." I arrived at her house fresh off tour and a five-hour drive to HB. She met me outside, invited me in and asked if I wanted to sit in the back yard and smoke a cigar? I said, "I would love to." We stayed up late around the fire and I answered every question she had for me. The following day were more questions from her lifelong best friend, Lisa, who was obviously checking on whether I was good enough for Tracy. She asked one thing only, "Stones or Beatles?" I replied, "Stones." I guess I passed. A chance introduction, one thing led to another, a few texts and phone calls later, and we've been together ever since.

The tour also included a night at a country bar in Thousand Oaks called the Borderline Bar and Grill. We had a decent crowd and had a great time playing that night. News hit about a mass shooting that took place there the week following our show. Some of the staff who were so generous and kind to us were amongst the thirteen people killed that night. It shook us as a band, being that we were just there the week prior. You never get used to hearing about mass shootings at music clubs or venues. This incident was just one year after the Route 91 Harvest music festival in Las Vegas where sixty-one people were killed and over eight hundred injured. Senseless acts of violence aimed at soft targets had people worried about who or where would be next.

In the fall of 2018, we played the Surf City Blitz in Huntington Beach. Over the two days, 40,000 friends and fans gathered on the beach for the giant show. Playing for our family at home was truly amazing. Jack still lives in HB today and Ron and I grew up there, so it meant a lot to us. The lineup was insane including, Bad Religion, Fear, Offspring, Social Distortion, Pennywise, Suicidal Tendencies, Voodoo Glow Skulls, Rancid, Interrupters, and more. It was a Cadillac of events and a great homecoming.

We played a couple of shows at The Regent in Hollywood with Youth Brigade and they sold out. It's always fun to play sold out shows close to home and see old friends. March 2019, we did another Musink Festival and followed that with shows at the Roxy and Garden Amphitheater in April. On July 31st we were off to Japan and Australia for the first time. We had never been to Australia or Japan, and I believe these countries were totally on all our bucket lists. The Australian dates were off the hook. Australia was like Orange County on steroids, great clubs, enthusiastic fans, and all the venues were packed! Australia is so big and sparsely populated, so we had to fly from city to city. Although we still managed to do some sightseeing and check out surf spots between flights. Japan was also amazing and another place I had always wanted to see. It was beautiful, calm, clean and orderly. Even the red-light district, where our hotel was located, had the air of controlled chaos. Businessmen out at night looking for women; it was like an organized strip club. I found it to be surreal, and it was quite the contrast to the parks, monuments, and temples peppered throughout the same city. It was ancient, serene, and beautiful, but also had the trappings of success.

September through November took us from San Diego playing the Casbah to The Glass House in Pomona, and then on to El Paso, Albuquerque, Phoenix, Tucson, and then Fort Collins, Colorado. In December, we played Riverside, Las Vegas, Bullhead City to Austin, then Dallas on December 31st.

LOVE AND LOSS

Early on we realized good equipment was important and vintage gear was the best. At the time it was fairly inexpensive, but still a lot for broke punk rockers, although by today's standards quite cheap. My first bass was a white Fender Music Master that I bought, new, for a few hundred dollars. I soon traded Steve Olson for a red mid 60's Music Master; he wanted the white one and I wanted the older one. Throughout this period, I played a few Fender Precisions and eventually I was able to upgrade again for a vintage white Rickenbacker 4001. I ended up painting it green or some awful color before painting it battleship grey. I should have left it alone; the bass deserved better. It was a bass that was made famous by bands such as Motorhead, The Jam, and possibly even Paul Gray of the Dammed. When Pat Brown and the boys went on an unauthorized shopping trip to a local music store one night, I suddenly had two brand new Ricky's 4001s to play. As I mentioned before, the giant plate glass windows were no match for golf clubs and crowbars. I also played or owned a few different P basses early on but favored the Rickenbackers.

During an early East Coast tour, I found my dream bass. I didn't know I had a dream bass before I saw my black Thunderbird at a store called Boston Music. I asked Jack if we had made any money on the tour so far, and he said, "Yes," so I took an advance on my pay and bought the 1976 black Thunderbird for $500 which became my main instrument for many years to come. Over the course of the years and hundreds of shows, I had broken it twice. I ended up having the headstock replaced once in San Francisco. Later in Long Beach, I added mother of pearl skull and crossbones inlays on the fret markers with a pearl band spelling out TSOL on the twelfth fret along with TSOL carved into the body; it was well played. I eventually had to replace the original pickups while on tour in New York with EMG pickups and played it for most of my career.

During the depths of my addiction, I ultimately lost the bass at a pawn shop in Southern California. I loved that bass and played it for many years. It went in and out of pawn shops towards the end when I was strung out until finally, I lost it. I had been waiting for a royalty check and when I went to pick it up at Westminster Jewelry and Loan, they had sold it; they were probably sick of my junkie shit. It was in a large custom built anvil case with TSOL painted on it. To this day, I think about that bass and the history it represented. I'm pretty sure someone in Orange County knows where it is or has it. I still feel the burn on that one, it will always be "the one that got away."

I've used several amps and cabinets over the years, an SVT cab is always a good choice if you're able to haul it around and don't mind its weight. I preferred GK heads and I still own two or three, some old and some newer. I've used Mesa Boogie Ampeg toward the end of the second TSOL; to my knowledge, I had the first two Jackson Thunderbirds ever made. Mike Eldred was running Jacksons custom shop and made me a black and white Thunderbird in which the white one had a reverse headstock. Mike also played in the "rock" version of TSOL for a short time and was probably the best sounding guitarist we had other than Ron. At one time I had four '76 Thunderbird basses, a white '76, two tobacco '76s, and my original black '76 with the skull and cross bones mother of pearl inlays.

Ron and I have been endorsed by Fender for quite a few years now. Ron even had his own model, an acoustic. The Country band, Midland said in an interview that Ron's guitar is the one they passed around on the porch while in the Teton Mountains when the band was born. Our rep and close friend, Michael Shultz, and Fender have always taken great care of us. Ron and I currently play Blonde vintage looking gear, Ron's is actually a mix of vintage and new. Mine is all new, but has been re-covered by Arab, our tech and old friend to look vintage. I mostly only use the full rig on local shows because of the size of the gear. We try to travel as light as possible when touring in the states. I generally use a Fender Solid State head with a Sands amp and a digital tuner in line with my Fender 6/10 cab or an 8/10 Fender style SVT when on the road.

I've thinned the herd over the last few years, but I still have 25 plus basses. Mostly Fender, some custom color P basses, a few vintage Fenders, a couple Jazz basses, a Gibson T bird, a vintage White Rick, a Music Man, a Yamaha fretless, a cool Fender acoustic bass with a TSOL pearl inlay on fret board, and last but not least, one of Ron's signature model acoustic guitars. I've made some poor choices over the years and let go of some classic vintage basses I wish I still had. Norm's Rare Guitars told me Nikki Sixx had purchased a rare custom color Jazz bass Ron found for me in the Midwest. I sold them during my divorce. I also sold a '61 P bass (the year I was born) that Murph from Sugar Ray was nice enough to sell to me, that one hurt! Good times.

The fact is, Flea, Nikki Sixx, and Adam Clayton, just to name a few, are some of the guys buying those kinds of instruments. Way out of my league moneywise, but for me and guys like me, every once in awhile, something cool drops into our laps. That's why it hurts all the more to let a good one slip away. I still consider myself quite lucky. After all, you can only play one at a time.

The search will continue for me, hopefully finding some of my old lost gems and possibly finding new pieces to the puzzle. Ron's collection and guitars found and lost, bought and sold over the years make my small effort seem insignificant at best. Ron has owned some amazing guitars. We will just have to wait for his book, but let's just say, his skill, knowledge, and eye for great guitars combined with his luck is unparalleled.

UNDER THE INFLUENCE

As a child the bass seemed to speak to me, and I love how the bass line can drive a song. To me, it's like the heartbeat of the music. I'm not aware of anyone in my family who played an instrument or had any musical background. I do remember my dad playing rock records pretty loudly in the house on Sunday race day and on the car radio. He enjoyed the music, and I could always tell he was in a good mood when it was turned up. As much as I enjoyed it, I didn't form an attachment to music until early punk rock and new wave. The way I came to hear punk rock was by listening to Rodney on the ROQ. I remember staying up late to catch Rodney's show on my clock radio. Tons of kids were listening to his late-night show and discovering music and bands we had never heard of before. Rodney was responsible for the launch and career of many great bands. His radio show was different from anything else. Essentially introducing punk rock, new wave, and glam bands to the LA scene.

To my ears and in my mind, punk was so different from anything that had come before. Punk rock got my attention and changed my life, it spoke to me. Bands from The Crowd to The Dickies and Weirdos, The Fly Boys, Devo, The Jam, The Dammed, Blondie, Sex Pistols, Buzzcocks, Sham 69, and Cockney Rejects. The music coming out was so new and unheard of; we would go to Zed Records in Long Beach to search for 45s not really knowing, at times, who the bands were. Between Ron, Bob, and myself we would get whatever looked interesting and we were bound to find a jewel. Zed's was one of the only places to get the music we were hearing on KROQ at the time. Mike who owned the place with his mom and brother was always cool and a nice guy. I remember seeing TSOL T-shirts hanging in the front window at one point and thought, "We Made It!" I promptly went inside and got him to give us a few. Small price for them to pay since they were bootlegged, and we never made any money from them. I for one was happy they were there at all. Zed's most certainly, in many ways, contributed to getting music by bands from across the pond into our hands. It was our lifeline to punk rock and alternative vinyl music at the time.

This was the second wave English invasion really, the first wave being the Beatles. Bands like Deep Purple, Led Zeppelin, Aerosmith, and so on didn't appeal to me. I was only exposed to it because that's what was playing on the radio at the time. It was like a friend's older brother's shit. However, over the years I have come to appreciate many styles of music. Obviously, I lean heavily on punk for my own musical style and taste, but I also like everything from Blues, R&B, Soul, Classical, and Classic Rock to some New Wave, and even a little country.

Some of my favorites include The Dammed, The Jam, Dickies, Weirdos, X, Siouxsie and The Banshees, and obviously Bowie. However, Elvis Costello influenced me greatly very early on and his bassist, Bruce Thomas was a standout in my mind. Bob Emory and I went to see him at Hollywood High School. R&B will always remain the heart and soul of bass driven music. James Jamerson was the uncredited bassist on most of the Motown hits and one of the best bass players of all time. He was a session player who wasn't totally recognized until he finally landed in the Rock n Roll Hall of Fame in 2020. Also included in this category would be Carol Kaye. She is estimated to have played on 10,000 recordings during her 50-year career. Marvin Gaye, Bill Withers, Lou Reed, Bob Marley, Peter Tosh, Jimmy Cliff, The Stones, Jimmy Hendrix, Stevie Ray Vaughan, AC/DC, and Johnny Cash, I hold in high regard and major musical influencers in my life.

TWENTY TWENTY

January of 2020 was to be a giant year for us, marking 40 years of our band. We were about to embark on a year-long tour to mark our 40th anniversary. We played a sold out show at The Observatory and toured the Pacific Northwest. Most, if not all, shows on this tour were sold out and the audiences were great. It was shaping up to be a good year of touring with Europe and the UK on the horizon. Against all odds and despite our past behavior, individual and collective trials, legal battles, and everything else we were celebrating our 40th anniversary!

As we embarked on what was to be the best year ever, we found ourselves at the Canadian border in mid-February. We had just played Seattle and approached the border with caution and anticipation. We hadn't been to Canada since the 80s and had been denied more than once. We had been told on no uncertain terms, if we tried to return, they would arrest us. The promotor had assured us everything would be okay and was taken care of. Through the proper channels, our visas were good, and we were ready to go. When we entered, they sat us down and made us wait for a while as they assisted other travelers. There seemed to be issues with some travelers ahead of us, so we waited our turn. We were invited up collectively, but then separated. Jack was taken to one corner of the counter to be interviewed and discuss his situation while the rest of us stood by for our turn. I was up next and was asked to step up to the counter. I was told that I did not have a visa, the band does not have a work visa, and based on our criminal records and despite our past efforts, we will not be allowed into Canada. Furthermore, we will never be getting into Canada. We were under the impression the promotor had everything in order and we were cleared, but apparently, once again, it wasn't the case.

Sadly, we're still paying for our past mistakes despite having changed our ways on almost every level. Actions have consequences, regardless of each of us having double digit years of sobriety, we are all still paying the price. In this particular case, our bad behavior in the past, although it feels like a world away, will stay with us till the day we die.

The unthinkable happened when Covid hit the US in February of 2020, or at least that's when we all became aware. We were heading home after a successful Pacific Northwest tour. We went home to the realization that something bad was happening and it was Covid. We had just left the state with the first breakout of the pandemic and were unaware of the full magnitude of what was to come. I thought I had the flu and didn't show enough of the symptoms to get tested, but with a 104 fever, no appetite, or sense of smell or taste, I went to urgent care. I was told they didn't have tests and to go home. I found myself entering a lockdown like everyone else. I was down and out for close to ten days. I didn't know how severe this was, but ultimately as the pandemic spread, it ended our 40-year anniversary tour.

In the coming weeks, I had to go back to California and move my girlfriend, Tracy out of her place in Huntington Beach. We decided she would make the permanent move to my home in Las Vegas.

Moving a three-car garage, four bedroom, three story house filled with furniture and a lot of dishes, I mean a lot, was a story in itself. In just two days we managed to get almost everything packed into a twenty-six-foot U-Haul. I made several trips to the Salvation Army. We were forced to leave bags outside the gate with "No Drop Off" signs, due to the shutdown. We worked all day and planned to leave as soon as the truck was filled. I drove while Tracy followed in my car, which was also packed full. We arrived in Las Vegas around midnight. Five hours, two hundred and sixty plus miles later, we finally made it home safely, that is, until I clipped a neighbor's car on the corner of my street. Turns out, you need to be extra careful while making a U-turn in a giant truck. The sound of the clip was more like a giant crash and brought the neighbors outside immediately. After an hour of exchanging information, we still had to unpack the U-Haul so we could return it in the morning. Not a scratch on it and thank God if it had been a foot longer the insurance wouldn't have paid for the neighbor's car repair. The car fell apart like a toy, by the way.

Immediately following this giant move, I also had the pleasure of relocating my aging mother from Arizona to Las Vegas which was very challenging during Covid. It was becoming clear the magnitude of which lives were being affected. The good news was we knew what we were doing having just mastered a move, but we had to do it all over again, and still during Covid. I was on a time constraint and had to pack up a four-bedroom house, sell what I could, and get her the essentials to move into a nursing home. She had two older dogs that keep her going and it was imperative they go with her. Finding a place to accept them was hard in itself, but during the pandemic it was even tougher. At one point when I had found her a home at the last minute, they decided they wouldn't take her dogs.

Driving back all night from Arizona with Tracy, my mom, her dogs, and trailer in tow it was looking like she would be staying with us. She didn't understand where she was going or where we were. The first morning she awoke asking questions about where she was, thinking she was in her house. She was calm but slightly confused and said it looked different. She slept on my couch downstairs for safety reasons, and with her dogs by her side, she was comfortable. We scrambled to find a new place while not being able to see it in person, as everything was closed. We enjoyed having my mom with us that week, but she needs professional care. Sadly, her dementia has left her with little or no short-term memory, but she talks about the old days with complete clarity. She is physically quite strong, but just unable to remember to care for herself, take her meds, and eat on her own. However, she did manage to put away several things I had out around the house. It took me a couple of days to find the missing items, a ceramic skull I had on the coffee table ended up in the trash. I found it funny she turned over coasters which have skulls on them; she said she didn't like them looking at her. Once I got her into a home, I had to visit my mom through a window for months and was only able to see her for a few short visits in person. I feel fortunate to have her settled, safe, and well cared for and got her there in the nick of time.

During the pandemic our band, like many others, had to find ways to continue working during the shutdown. I believe we were one of the first bands to do a live feed show for Big Daddy Carlos, a long-time friend and club owner in Las Vegas. He had the idea to do a virtual concert with no audience and minimal crew. We met at his club, Backstage Bar & Billiards on May 24, 2020, and filmed one of the first live streamed shows. Nothing compares to playing live, nothing. The atmosphere, energy, and direct interaction with the audience is what TSOL has always been about. In my opinion recordings and records are just a vehicle to the live show. The event was an attempt to try and stay connected with our fans and a safe alternative.

The following months and into 2021 were spent mostly in lockdown. No one had any idea the pandemic would last so long. We stayed home and isolated while we witnessed the world becoming a dark and lonely place with no end in sight. Just when a store or restaurant would re-open, it was soon closed again. We masked up and tried to stay positive. Tracy and me managed to take small road trips, daily drives, and walk in the open air. We took a few days and went to my favorite fishing spot in Utah where I had taken Tracy shortly after we met. We both love it there. It's a sort of reset for me, away from the city and all its distractions.

In February 2021, I returned to Huntington Beach to film my segment for a long-awaited documentary called Ignore Heroes that Jack was directing. Going back to Huntington Beach where it all started for Ron and me, and where Jack currently resides, feels like home. At the time I thought I would finally be able to see my bandmates, but due to the pandemic we were there on separate days. We had to get tested for Covid to be allowed to film at all, and only a few people could be on set at a time.

Although we weren't playing during this time, we continued to speak often, and we were all looking forward to things getting back to normal. Like many other bands we were eager to get out and play again without restrictions. There has never been a time in history where live music became essentially non-existent.

AGAINST ALL ODDS

Addiction, jail, prison, self-destruction, legal battles, lost guitars, lost jobs, lost homes, loss of freedom and friends, failed marriages, Father Time, and even a virus can't seem to stop the mighty TSOL. After all, if we couldn't destroy TSOL ourselves, I don't believe anything else can. With good luck or good karma or possibly God's good grace, three of my original bandmates are still with me, and I with them. With these giants by my side, we have managed to overcome many things. Despite the setbacks and obstacles put in our way, whether brought on by ourselves or others, we have stuck together. None of this would have been possible without sobriety. I'm forever grateful for my bandmates and the twelve-step program for the life I have today.

Thinking back on my life and where I am, to be here, present, alive and well, to still be able to play music, I am honored. The body of work TSOL has created will live on forever. Despite not being commercially recognized on a large scale, I think our contribution will stand the test of time. The bands, artists, and musicians who site us as one of their influences truly makes me feel honored. I'm proud of the legacy that TSOL leaves behind and the music we continue to produce today. I'm grateful for where I am, who I am with, and what my life has become.

Jack, Ron, Greg, and I, being the original members, are still actively writing, recording, and touring after forty plus years. I don't know what other band can say that today. The only one who is not with us is Todd, the one who passed away (RIP). We added our fearless and talented drummer, Antonio in 2017. He's been a great asset for TSOL and a pleasure to play with.

We played a few shows throughout the remainder of 2021. Each show reminding me of how lucky I am to be able to still do what I love. To be among friends and see familiar faces through the years. The faces of friends and fans who continue to show up, support, and be there with me, for us, means everything. A small moment in time, but memories that will last forever.

Life is balance, life is gratitude, life is a gift. — M.R.

IN CLOSING
GIANTS

I can't say enough about my original bandmates and the immense talent and creativity that each one has contributed to the band. I am truly grateful for each and every one of you, as you have been a source of strength and inspiration throughout my journey. Thank you from the bottom of my heart. It's not often a band remains intact despite the ups and downs, especially over 40 years, but today they still remain my best friends and brothers till the end.

Jack Grisham is still the fearless and charismatic ringleader today as he was when we started TSOL 40 plus years ago. He is the ultimate front man with his knowledge and understanding of music and what he wants and how to get it. He is as unafraid as he ever was to push the envelope and break the mold. As a writer, author, and director, he is one of the most talented people I know. This needs to be said, even though he probably won't like it. In my opinion, Jack is selfless, caring, and kind. He is willing to help people anytime, day or night.

Todd Barnes was a unique drummer with influences as diverse from punk to metal, from Iron Maiden and Motorhead to The Damned and Rush. Todd had a rough exterior, but a gentle soul. He was funny, friendly, wild, and a solid and loyal friend. He was taken too soon, and I miss him.

Ron Emory's sound, tone, attack, and creativity are unparalleled! No one sounds like Ron! Best friends aside, he is my favorite guitarist and one of the reasons I still enjoy playing live so much. When we're in the pocket, we're unstoppable. That said, aside from the band, Ron and his wife, Gia have played a huge part in their community, creating a successful outreach music program with their Conservatory. They successfully teach music to kids and adults who may not have had the opportunity otherwise. I have mad respect and love for Ron and his family.

Last, but not least I must mention another true gentleman that we met and we recruited as a very young man. I don't think that his parents were that pleased on our first visit. Greg Kuehn has been an asset from day one. *Beneath the Shadows* would not exist had Greg not joined TSOL. His talent as a writer, composer, multi-instrumentalist, and producer makes him quite a force. However, to me, the best thing about Greg, is who he is as a man. He is a father, husband, and great friend. Greg said it best in reference to TSOL's dynamic, "When you have magic, you can't take it for granted."

MORE ABOUT THE BOOK

Like they say in Coney Island, this is a dark ride a kind of a noir memoir that's ultimately a tale of love, loss, loyalty, and redemption. A must read and unlike most books of this ilk, it's ALL TRUE!
   —**Mark Mahoney, American Tattoo Artist**

Oh, hell yeah, this Mike Roche history lesson is really happening! A fast paced read at the same tempo of songs he and his co-conspirators created. From growing up a typical Southern California skater and surfer kid to getting involved with a bunch of young delinquents and making a wild hairball detour to start his brush with a few showbiz scuzz bags. He takes us along on some twists and turns and exposes the cuts, bruises and scars of his romp through life.
   — **Keith Morris, frontman for the Circle Jerks, OFF!, and Flag**

I Play With Giants is an interesting title considering Mike was the tallest of all of us! I get it though, the rockers have John Entwistle from the Who, the blues have Willie Dixon, the Mods have Bruce Foxton of the Jam, Motown has James Jameson, jazz has Stanley Clarke, funk has Bootsie and Flea, punk rock has Chuck Dukouski, Matt Freeman, and on the other side of the pond, Paul Grey, Sid Vicious, Paul Simonon and Algy Ward. All giants in their field without any question… however, my best friend of almost 50 years, Mike Roche is our giant! And I would put him up against any of them! With a style all his own, original and as low as you can go or as high as you can take it, his bass lines are such a huge part of TSOL's sound… punchy, driving and moving through the songs start to finish. This is what allows the rest of us to play with our giant!!! I love Mike dearly with everything I've got!
   — **Ron Emory, Original Guitar Player, TSOL**

Mike Roche was the guy I talked to when booking TSOL. He was always the consummate gentleman. I found it a pleasure to deal with him and we became friends. He's just a good guy and well deserved of any success this book may bring him. His story is a must read for all TSOL fans. He has been to hell and back and has survived with class. I love Mike Roche! Buy his book.
   — **Jerry Roach, Owner/OG Punk Rock Promoter of the Cuckoo's Nest**

I love Mike! I first met him when TSOL came over to my house in Santa Barbara in 1981. We sat in my backyard and had a wonderful conversation about cacti. It was the day of Goldenvoice's very first concert and they were headlining. The show that night was crazy! And the after party at the hotel where TSOL was staying was even crazier! Mike has always been the kind of guy who's trustworthy and dependable in tense situations. He has your back!

I remember in 1982 we had a meeting with TSOL and the Dead Kennedys at the On Broadway office in San Francisco. When we finished and walked out, we saw that the group of people I had come up with were being harassed by 10 skinheads outside the club. Mike immediately rushed into action and got in the middle of all the skinheads. They recognized who he was and they backed down completely. He was a guy who you always wanted on your side!
— **Gary Tovar, Goldenvoice founder**

When I first came to Southern California, Mike and Ron were two of the first people I became friends with. Mike and I quickly bonded over our love of music and motorcycles. Mike was the master of tone and style, but my favorite quality of Mike's is fearlessness to speak directly and not worry about what other people think. He has been a giant influence on me through the 40 plus years we have been friends. I owe much gratitude to Mike for what I have become. I love you brother! God bless Mike and True Sounds of Liberty.
— **Mike "Cheese" Brown**

HONORABLE MENTIONS
In no particular order

Drummers who played with TSOL
Antonio Val Hernandez
Anthony "Tiny" Biuso
Billy Blaze
Chip Hanna
Chris Lagorford (RIP)
Danny
Jamie Reidling
Jay O'Brien
Matt
Tim
Travis

ACKNOWLEDGMENTS

I would like to take a moment to express my sincerest appreciation to Tracy, my amazing girlfriend. I am beyond grateful for the love and unwavering support you have given me while writing my story. From the early days of our relationship, you have been my rock, my confidante, and my biggest cheerleader. Your passion and encouragement have helped me overcome countless obstacles, and your continuous love and care for both me and our beloved Ro have made every day brighter. Tracy, I cannot thank you enough for being the light in my life. I love you more than words could ever express.

To my editor, Melissa Elhardt, thank you for your expertise and attention to detail. You have played a pivotal role in improving the clarity of my writing. Without you, I would never have known how poor my grammar was.

I would like to express my heartfelt gratitude to my publisher and dear friend, Iris Berry at Punk Hostage Press. Your trust in me and unwavering enthusiasm for this book have been invaluable. You have taught me to trust the process and not to rush my story. Your willingness to take on this project without any hesitation means the world to me.

To my friends, family, and fans who have been part of my life, past, present, or future, thank you from the bottom of my heart:
Arab Eric Groff, Bill Hardy, Blaze James, Bob Dixon, Bob Emory, Bob Hurley, Brandon Rezza, "Dexter" Holland, Brian Cullen, Bud Llamas, Chris Grayson (RIP), Chuk Davis & Bugg, Cindy Brewer-McKitrick, (Vraney), Coleen & Greg Dunbar, Danny Cameron, Dean Cleary, Doug Hoffman, Duff McKagen, Dwight Dunn, Ed Marshall, Edward Colver, Fletcher, Freddie Perrault, Gary Tovar, Gerry "Taters" Hurtato (RIP), Jack Rabbit, Jerry Meyling Small, Jerry Roach, Jim "Jimbo" Barker, Joe Escalante, Joe Wood, Kevin "Noodles" Wasserman, Landon Gale-George, Lindsay Carmichael, Mark Mahoney, Michael Schulz and Fender, Mike De La Cruz, Mike Eldred, Mike Martt (RIP), Mike Rubin, Mike Vraney (RIP), Otis "O" Barthoulameu (RIP), Pat Downey, Paul Tollette, Steve Cunningham, Steve "Humann" Pfauter (RIP), Stevo Jensen (RIP), Steve Reehl (RIP).

— **Much love and respect, MR.**

MORE ABOUT THE AUTHOR

Mike Roche is a founding member and bassist of the legendary punk rock band TSOL. Formed in 1978 in Long Beach, CA, the band have toured the world and appeared in several movies which included the 1984 Penelope Spheeris' film Suburbia, where the band did a live performance. A surfer kid from Orange County, Mike was instrumental in bringing punk rock fashion to downtown HB. Mike created and managed, The Electric Chair downtown on Main St., (The first punk rock store in HB.) Mike is also a professional tattooist who earned his apprenticeship at the famous Mark Mahoney's Shamrock Social Club on the Sunset Strip. He has worked for Hart & Huntington Tattoo since shortly after their opening at The Palms Casino. Today Mike resides in Las Vegas Nevada, where he lives with his girlfriend, Tracy and their rescue dog, an Akita named Rowan. Mike continues to play with three of the original founding members of TSOL, and if you're lucky, you may just get him to tattoo you!

MORE BOOKS ON PUNK HOSTAGE PRESS

Danny Baker
Fractured – 2012

A Razor
Better Than a Gun in A Knife Fight – 2012 Drawn Blood: Collected Works From D.B.P.LTD., 1985–1995 - 2012 Beaten Up Beaten Down – 2012 Small Catastrophes in A Big World – 2012 Half-Century Status – 2013 Days of Xmas Poems – 2014 Puro Purismo – 2021

Iris Berry
The Daughters of Bastards – 2012
All That Shines Under the Hollywood Sign – 2019
The Trouble with Palm Trees – 2021
Gas Station Etiquette – 2022

Yvonne De la Vega
Tomorrow, Yvonne - Poetry & Prose for Suicidal Egoists – 2012

Carolyn Srygley-Moore
Miracles Of the Blog: A Series– 2012

Rich Ferguson
8th & Agony – 2012

Jack Grisham
Untamed – 2013
Code Blue: A Love Story ~ Limited Edition – 2014 – Paperback – 2020
Pulse of the World. Arthur Chance, Punk Rock Detective – 2022

Dennis Cruz
Moth Wing Tea – 2013
The Beast Is We – 2018

Frank Reardon
Blood Music – 2013

Pleasant Gehman
Showgirl Confidential – 2013
Rock 'N' Roll Witch: A Memoir of Sex Magick, Drugs, And Rock 'N' Roll – 2022

Hollie Hardy
How To Take a Bullet and Other Survival Poems – 2014

SB Stokes
History Of Broken Love Things – 2014

Michele McDannold
Stealing The Midnight from A Handful of Days – 2014

Joel Landmine
Yeah, Well... – 2014
Things Change – 2022

MORE BOOKS ON PUNK HOSTAGE PRESS

A.D. Winans
Dead Lions – 2014

S.A. Griffin
Dreams Gone Mad with Hope – 2014
Pandemic Soul Music – 2022

Nadia Bruce-Rawlings
Scars – 2014
Driving in The Rain – 2020

Lee Quarnstrom
WHEN I WAS A DYNAMITER, Or, how a Nice Catholic Boy Became a Merry Prankster, a Pornographer, and a Bridegroom Seven Times – 2014

Alexandra Naughton
I Will Always Be Your Whore/Love Songs for Billy Corgan – 2014
You Could Never Objectify Me More Than I've Already Objectified Myself – 2015

Maisha Z Johnson
No Parachutes to Carry Me Home – 2015

Michael Marcus
#1 Son and Other Stories – 2017

Danny Garcia
LOOKING FOR JOHNNY, The Legend of Johnny Thunders – 2018

William S. Hayes
Burden of Concrete – 2020

Todd Moore
Dillinger's Thompson – 2020

Dan Denton
$100-A-Week Motel – 2021

Jack Henry
Driving W/ Crazy, living with madness – 2021

Joe Donnelly
So Cal: Dispatches from the End of The World – 2022

Patrick O'Neil
Anarchy at The Circle K – On the Road with Dead Kennedys, TSOL, Flipper, Subhumans and... Heroin – 2022

Richard Modiano
The Forbidden Lunchbox – 2022

Shawna Kenney
I Was A Teenage Dominatrix 3rd Edition – 2023

O.R.
Ophelia Rising – 2023

www.ingramcontent.com/pod-product-compliance
Lightning Source LLC
Chambersburg PA
CBHW031631160426
43196CB00006B/372